THE
MOBILE
SOCIETY

THE
MOBILE
SOCIETY

A History of the Moving and Storage Industry

JOHN HESS

McGRAW-HILL BOOK COMPANY

New York   St. Louis   San Francisco   Düsseldorf   Johannesburg
Kuala Lumpur   London   Mexico   Montreal
New Delhi   Panama   Rio de Janeiro
Singapore   Sydney   Toronto

Library of Congress Cataloging in Publication Data

Hess, John, 1931–
    The mobile society.

    1. Storage and moving trade—United States—
History. 2. Moving, Household. I. Title.
HE5623.H47   388.3'24   72-8486
ISBN 0-07-028420-2

1234567890 BPBP 76543

*The editors for this book were W. Hodson Mogan and Don A.
Douglas, the designer was Naomi Auerbach, and its production
was supervised by Teresa F. Leaden. It was set in Alphatype
Caledo by University Graphics, Inc.*

It was printed and bound by The Book Press.

Contents

Foreword

The moving and storage industry is big; it is a one-and-a-half to two-billion dollar industry. It is diverse. It works directly with many kinds of customers. It packs, it stores, it moves to and from the home or office. It uses mainly trucks, but water, air, and other modes may be used, and it serves the needs of families and individuals as well as large and small corporations and government. But in spite of its millions of customers, few know much about it. That is the big *why* of this industry history.

And there is a special reason to record industry history at this time. While the moving and storage industry is an old industry, its modern form evolved during the highway and trucking revolutions. Participants who shaped the industry are now being replaced by younger professionals. This is the time to ask these leaders to reflect on industry progress, and it is the time to provide background for people who are just becoming a part of the industry, as well as for the general public and for those who are the close clients of the industry.

The National Moving & Storage Technical Foundation was the catalyst in sponsoring *The Mobile Society*. The Technical

Foundation sponsors research for the entire moving and storage industry in this country. A primary aim is helping the industry develop its full potential in terms of serving the public in the most innovative, creative, and efficient manner.

The Foundation was able to gain the assistance of the author John Hess, who has an extensive background in preparing historical material. Under a Foundation research grant, Mr. Hess was given a free hand both in his research and in his writing. The opinions expressed and conclusions reached are those of Mr. Hess based on his observations, feelings, and analyses. While they are not necessarily those of the Foundation or necessarily those of the industry, it is felt that he has achieved the objectives for the book as envisioned by the Foundation.

Preface

A word about the scheme of writing this popular history is in order. Perhaps it is best to state what the book is not intended to be. It is not meant to be a "how-to" guide for the housewife, for example, because several books with just that purpose in mind have been published in the last few years, one very recently. Also, it was thought that a busy housewife would not consult a history of a particular industry in order to learn about ways to improve the efficiency of her move. Of course, if the background contained here helps in the communication process between mover and customer, then the time is well spent. Any author is grateful for a reader who has learned something from anything that he has written, no matter what the original purpose.

Some of the best examples of this kind of instructional publishing are: *The Home Encyclopedia of Moving Your Family,* by Margaret Randall, Berkley Publishing Corporation, New York; and *Moving: A Common Sense Guide to Relocating Your Family,* by Edith Ruina, Funk & Wagnalls Company, New York. Also, *Help Your Family Make a Better Move,* by Helen

Giammattei and Kay Slaughter, Doubleday & Company, Inc., Garden City, N.Y., has been well known in the industry for several years.

In researching the available materials relating to the moving and storage industry, I have used especially the back issues of *The Furniture Warehouseman,* the moving and storage industry's professional journal, whose files have served as valuable sources for information about the early days.

This exciting business has grown from the simplest beginnings to huge proportions, affecting almost one out of every four people in the United States each year. The prospects for the future are for even greater prosperity and growth.

However, this book is basically a *history* of past events in the moving and storage industry in America, with some predictions and analyses of future possibilities. Information of a different nature, covering helpful hints about moving and storage matters, is available in the form of easy-to-read pamphlets provided to interested customers by movers throughout the country.

John Hess

THE
MOBILE
SOCIETY

1

The Mobile Society

Whenever an American reporter goes to Europe or to South America, people always ask him the same question: "Why do Americans move so much, why are they so restless, why do people change things around so much in your country?"

One might say that we are still pioneers, wanting to better ourselves, able to move over our excellent roads and not hampered by the past. Also, Americans are well-known for looking toward the future because the future has always seemed unlimited in this country. Why, all you have to do is go around the corner to find a better job . . . and some day many of us will even set foot on the moon. . . .

Another partial answer to our foreign friends' question is the fabled American affluence, our ability to make the most of opportunities that an older society has not had in any form. Therefore, the growth of such a dynamic society has very directly affected and improved the position of the American moving and storage industry, which so contributes to the mobility of this country.

1

For example, this mobility of people is clearly brought to mind when one thinks of two particularly important historical events in the last thirty years, or roughly one generation of American life. "Where was I?" one might ask. "What was I doing? Where was I when I heard the news?" The two events in question are the bombing of Pearl Harbor on December 7, 1941, and the assassination of John F. Kennedy on November 22, 1963.

Many dates could be chosen at random, but the essential point is that today eight out of every fifteen people are residing in a different town from the one they were in when these important events took place.

We live through the lives of the great and our lives become part of theirs. When the Kennedys moved to 1600 Pennsylvania Avenue they used the Merchants Transfer and Storage Company of Washington, D.C., a venerable firm whose owner remembered storing household goods for the Kennedys for years. Mr. John Newbold said on that happy day: "The Kennedys have been customers of ours for a number of years and we are still holding items in storage for them. Needless to say, we felt honored to have been selected to perform this service."

This anecdote shows how the moving and storage business is really a part of everything that people do right up to the top rung of our political and social structure. When Lyndon Johnson left the White House in 1969, the Security Storage Company of Washington, headed by Philip Larner Gore, was there to do the job. At the same time, in New York City, the household goods of Richard M. Nixon were being handled by highly trained professionals of the Beverly Storage Co., who worked for three days packing the goods in Mr. Nixon's Fifth Avenue apartment before moving them to the famous address that Lyndon Johnson was just vacating. A representative of Mr. Nixon watched every mover's action and closed-circuit television cameras scanned the apartment's elevator doors. The owner of the moving company, Mr. Sidney Kandel, supervised every detail of the move. Too much was at stake to make a mistake.

When everything was carefully packed, a trusted veteran driver pulled a moving van up to the service entrance of the apartment house, and possessions were loaded aboard with great attention. Later that same day the van pulled into a security-guarded parking space not far from the White House. The next morning, again under heavy guard, the goods were successfully transported to the new address. The occupant of the White House and his family were said to have been extremely pleased with the final results.

However, the moves of those famous families are only a part of this dynamic industry—there are the corporate moves, the moves of enormously complicated equipment, the unusual move, the simple move, the beautifully handled move, the problem move. Somehow, though, there is always action and thus interest about the most fascinating element on earth—people —and what motivates them.

Actually, we really don't know the reasons behind all moves. This complexity makes for variety and so no day is quite like another. No move is quite the same as another, a situation making for a minimum of boredom and an inability to predict what will happen next.

Public relations plays a big part in this business. Take Disneyland in California: Someone had to move the materials and equipment into those imaginative buildings. Whether you think it silly or beautiful or the eighth wonder of the world, Disneyland is an outstanding advertisement for our country, and Global Van Lines helped to make it all possible as official movers for the project. Even foreign dignitaries made a special effort to see it, while avoiding other, less pleasant visiting opportunities during their stays in this country.

In the first ten months of 1956, more than two million people were able to see a re-created 1890-style moving van, which was supplied by Bekins Moving and Storage Company. This horse-drawn wagon was made available to anyone who wanted "intramural" travel in the Disney enclosures. What was most important was that people who came and saw this unique team and equipment might remember the name of its sponsor enough to choose it in the future.

The moving industry has been growing increasingly conscious of this area of personal relations, and as that late genius, Walt Disney, said, "I'm pleased whenever I look at this quaint exhibit that tells a whole story of dreams come true in one building and a horse-drawn cart." That statement made by Mr. Disney could apply very directly to the moving and storage industry's history, an account of American ingenuity; but that is a very complicated story which takes a certain time to tell.

Almost every adult—art fan or not—remembers the *Mona Lisa's* visit to the New York World's Fair in 1964. What many people have never realized is that this fabulous treasure was insured for under $100—and there were no claims, no losses after the move was completed. This famous work was uninsurable.

Also in 1964 occurred the equally famous move of another *objet d'art:* Michelangelo's famous creation, the Pietá, was shipped from Vatican City to New York, where it was successfully handled by the McNally Brothers firm of Brooklyn, New York. Actually, moving the 6,700-pound marble structure of the Virgin Mary holding the body of Christ was awaited with some anxiety on both sides of the Atlantic. Many European art lovers were especially skeptical that the famous art object could be safely transported, and insisted that the most traditional and safest methods known to man be used—a heavy wooden crate, wood shavings, paper, and excelsior. (Who can ever forget excelsior sitting in the corners of Victorian houses for years as a memory of *one* past move in the family's history?) This idea was firmly opposed by an American committee of shipping experts, headed by John T. Murray, Vice-president of McNally Brothers. The committee finally decided on a closed-cell, expansible plastic material for packing, with a steel shipping container for handling and exterior protection. The particularly plastic material, called "Dylite," was manufactured by Koppers Company, Pittsburgh, Pennsylvania, and at the time was almost unknown in Italy. The material can come in beaded form, like tiny pearls, and in 2-inch-thick slabs.

Before packing, the statue was x-rayed and photographed with cobalt 60, so that hidden flaws might be discovered and interior damage, no matter how slight, could be detected. Unlike the *Mona Lisa*, this shipment was insured for $6 million.

Then the precious piece was put on a plywood-topped base and a wooden container was placed around it. For every 2 feet of planking, plywood lining was affixed to the interior walls. The statue was then completely immersed in beads and encompassed by Dylite slab, and the crate was sealed. A low-bed McNally trailer met the statue in New York and proceeded at the mammoth speed of 3 miles an hour to the site of the World's Fair — not unusual for rush-hour travelers who often don't go any faster than that anyway at 6 P.M. on the Van Wyck Expressway.

The whole point is that American technology and care have developed greatly since the idea that every move involved the old family piano, scarred and gouged . . . and left to dry or rot in the sun and rain of some lonely delivery deck. American moving has come a long way since then, and the millions of people who saw what is probably the world's most famous art object were given this pleasure by a rapidly advancing moving technology.

Improvement and advancement in the eyes of the public, as well as in the mind of the professional himself, were not restricted to art. The world of the possible — politics — saw the same efficiency starting to show itself. In 1956 the eyes of the world were on President Dwight Eisenhower and his entourage as it unloaded in San Francisco for that year's Republican National Convention. It was San Francisco's City Transfer that whisked its bright and efficient vans up to the planes as soon as the television lights had disappeared to carry away the bags of the entire Eisenhower party.

Equally interesting stories took place in other walks of life. Small but very important events are constantly happening that show the moving industry's important role in the lives of both the great and the ordinary of this world. On the bustling Pennsylvania Turnpike, at the same time that John Kennedy's assassination was taking place in Dallas, a station wagon and a van representing the M. F. Rockey Storage Company, New Cumberland, Pennsylvania, were giving urgent treatment to some very precious cargo—the life of a 12-year-old boy, Bobby Cassell, who had to travel anywhere he went in an iron lung. Bobby was being transported to a hospital just outside Pittsburgh in Leetsdale, Pennsylvania.

The test of whether this move was successful was very clear: if the boy was without mechanical assistance in breathing for more than one minute, he would be dead. The dangerous journey was completed in six hours, and a doctor and a nurse were in attendance at all times. Prior to 1963 this kind of transport was attempted only once before in the nation's history and this was the first in the state of Pennsylvania. The move was supervised by Robert H. Rife, President of the Rockey Company.

No matter how delicate the person or product to be moved, the industry has grown into its responsibilities and has been accomplishing a tremendous job of image improvement over the years.

The examples are endless, as complex as the very life that the industry serves: a half-million-dollar shipment of eighteenth-century yellow glazed English earthenware was successfully transported, during the middle of the 1960's, with the help of tons of Puffed Rice. Each china barrel on its way to the Smithsonian Institution in Washington, D.C., was packed in a wooden crate with 4 inches of clearance on all six sides. The gaps, and there were plenty of them, were filled with Puffed Rice cereal for additional final cushioning.

Not always have these moves been made on the ground. Whole families have been moved by air by the Security Storage Company of Washington, D.C., for instance, and other major operators throughout the country. One year a retiring Washington man of some means bought an estate in the Virgin Islands and gathered his furniture, his servants, his pets, and his entire family and flew off like the wind. Many people are able to do this in these affluent times, but the decisions are affected by several factors.

In the corporate sector, for example, some companies have found it is economical to have their employees' goods shipped by air when the families are going overseas. Most companies pay per diem rates to their transferred families and have found that fast air shipment will cut down on the number of days that must be paid for while a family waits for its household goods. The old adage of "time means money" is very true in this area, where the cost of the air movement of household goods is higher than surface shipment, but the overall charges for the transfer of an entire household, including per diem costs, may not be.

In the governmental sector, opportunities for moving and storage companies have been endless. For example, the Davidson Transfer and Storage Company of Baltimore found itself in the middle of one of its biggest challenges when it won a government contract recently to move Social Security records. In one weekend, the firm handled 5,000,000 pounds of files of information on which the Social Security System is based. Without Davidson's help, perhaps few of us would ever enjoy a happy old age.

In the academic sector, City Transfer of San Francisco was called upon to move the Stanford University Medical School. A newspaper photograph of Stanford's medical skeletons being transported is a priceless part of the industry's history.

On the domestic scene some moves are more challenging than others. The Phoenix branch of the Lyon Van and Storage Company literally reached the bottom one time during the 1960's—it got to the floor of the Grand Canyon, ending up 5,000 feet below the canyon's rim at the remote Indian Village of Supai, Arizona.

Starting with the most modern methods of road van and packing services, the firm agreed to transport the worldly goods of Mr. and Mrs. Gabriel Sharp. Mr. Sharp is a full-blooded Mohave Indian and his wife, Gail, was to teach at Supai's only school—her students being all Indian children. The move originated in Scottsdale, Arizona, and at the south rim of the canyon the party was met by a 15-mule pack train. Heavy items were flown in by helicopter. Because of the limited carrying capacities of the mules, no carton could weigh more than 50 pounds. The move was quite successful and the Sharps set up housekeeping, with Mrs. Sharp teaching and Mr. Sharp acting as a law-enforcement official for the United States Bureau of Indian Affairs.

Companies dealing with metropolitan storage assignments have also had their challenges. There have been problems with rioting, when people couldn't even get to their places of business. If you have been on 14th Street during the early 1970's in Washington, you can still see the effects of the riots on buildings lining that street.

In other parts of the country conditions were equally difficult. A quietly descriptive statement by a Detroit warehouseman during the 1967 riots sums up very well the experience of the industry at that time: "When I was getting ready to go to the warehouse on that Monday morning, I heard over the radio a warning for all people to stay off the streets. However, I went down to the office, encountering practically no traffic. On arrival, I found that the area was very quiet except for police cars, National Guard vehicles and fire trucks beating a path on Grand Avenue, a thoroughfare that is about 100 feet from the office window. . . ." Even in fiercely law-and-order Milwaukee, the situation was just as hazardous. Said an eyewitness to the disturbances of that year, "We were not able to reach our office and warehouse even to *check* conditions, answer phones, or secure the building. The entire metropolitan area was under the National Guard protection and curfew." Most shipments scheduled to be sent to the city were rerouted and no attempt was even made to enter the troubled zones.

The implications for other cities were just as dire. In Newark, New Jersey, for example, the local chamber of commerce was forced to institute a telephone squad of volunteers who were given the numbers of key executives who had to be called about conditions when the riots started. These executives were indispensable to their firms and had to make the crucial decision of whether to come down to the warehouse or not. Often millions of dollars of equipment were at stake.

The implications to the experienced businessman who is primarily engaged in valuable storage are many. As Philip Larner Gore said recently: "Many people are simply not taking their fine things back home after a summer's storage, for instance, preferring to take the chance with the professional storage man rather than risk that their best collections of china and silver will be taken or damaged by individual criminals breaking into their homes here in the Washington area."

The responsibility on center-city professional storage specialists is great: in higher insurance costs, in threatened violence to employees—and particularly in increased costs of precautionary measures. One extreme example of protection is a warehouse of stone, like one recently constructed to combat our violent times.

The Security Terminals Warehouse of Springfield, Missouri, is one of the most durable and fire-resistant warehouses ever known to man, at least since the Egyptians. The features are not possible for all buildings, of course, but consider the specifications: 50-foot-thick ceilings, solid stone inside and outside walls, unlimited floor lead capacity. The warehouse is actually a cave, or a mine, carved out of solid limestone. This storage facility has become an impenetrable fortress in a troubled country.

The American warehouseman has risen to the challenge, however, and will continue to accept this increased responsibility in the years ahead.

Other countries have their troubles, too, showing how moving men, somehow, can cope with almost anything. After the Berlin Wall went up during the early part of the decade, the moving industry's problems increased tenfold in a country already famous for its hard life. A German shipper who also happens to be a German National, in order to move between West and East Germany must, first, prove that he has been a resident of West Berlin since 1954 without interruption. Secondly, he must provide the authorities with a complete list of the household goods to be transported, *stating the make and number of all electrical appliances.* A special list for books and records must be compiled. To add to these difficulties, the West Berlin Senate has prescribed that certain books and records cannot be shipped under any circumstances. The red tape that these shippers tolerate is hard to imagine for the average American who moves from state to state with relative freedom.

Further, the shipper in Germany must accompany his belongings, which are inspected at numerous border checkpoints before entering the Communist *Deutsche Democratische Republic.* Like bureaucratic workers everywhere, these guards can inflict out of their own frustration or just plain nastiness, meticulous searches at any one of the countless checkpoints, where the entire van may be unloaded for an examination of the contents.

However, not many people have to contend with the moving of an *entire city* — which is what the Brazilian government tried and successfully completed at the beginning of the 1960's in an amazing combination of hard work and animal courage.

In Brazil there are office buildings that have been under construction for ten or more years without being completed, while on the roof of the building a night club operates, the only part of the building that is making a profit.

Under these ground rules in this Latin country, the enormous job that Brazil's NFWA member, *Transportes Fink,* successfully completed in the Brasilia moving operation is even more amazing. The workmen for the firm were forced to carry the heaviest office equipment up ten flights of stairs because elevators had not been made operational yet. For weeks these workmen had been on 16-hour work days. Two companies, using 600 to 800 trucks, two airplanes and a busline, were available to add to the *Fink* manpower. An initial contingent of 2,000 people had gathered together in an arid plateau, 4,000 feet above the Brazilian jungle in this new city called Brasilia — this number grew to more than 100,000 people in the short span of a few years. It was simply the successful transportation of *all* essential people and services to Brasilia — the making of a new capital. This must certainly rank as one of the most colossal moves in history.

Although the extraordinary moves described above are dramatic and colorful, much more numerous are the ordinary and basic moves from point A to point B, the move of the ordinary American family and the business office move that produce the problems and satisfactions that come from doing one's job well day-by-day in a consistent way. These fruits of labor are not always easy to come by, for people have problems when they move and the moving man must cope with these problems — and he usually does. There are questions of estimating versus final costs, the problems of scheduling to the satisfaction of the customer, the settling of claims, all the hard questions that one hears so much about in these days of "consumerism." To illustrate how these experiences can relate to our history, let us take an average move from point A to point B and see how the ordinary, average American family is using the services of the widespread moving and storage industry.

The people who are using these moving and storage services are becoming increasingly sophisticated and educated, just as the moving and storage men are becoming more professional as the years go on. A *Newsweek* magazine survey of 1,110 subscribing families who had moved in 1969 shows an interesting portrait of Americans. For example, the average income of this typical family using a van line for moving its household goods was $17,334.00 in 1969. Of these family units, the head of the household was a professional man in 29.5% of the cases studied; a manager, a corporate official, or a proprietor in

18.6% of the examples used; and a sales person 21.2% of the time.

Of those households studied in the *Newsweek* survey, the man of the house was a college graduate in 51.9% of the examples considered. Another 8.3% had attended college and 9.6% were high school graduates.

As the figures show, this is an educated and highly paid group of people who expect a good share of service for the money put out on their movement of household goods. The moving and storage operator must adjust to this new kind of customer, rendering service satisfactory in every way. The reasons are obvious: repeat business in the mobile society is critical to the profit growth of any company in the moving and storage industry, large or small.

The industry reports on service, again in this age of heavy consumer response, have been relatively good. The same *Newsweek* survey showed that 60.4% of the people responding to the survey would use the same moving company again for their next move. The challenges for the future of the moving and storage industry, and the need for more professional performance from original estimating to final claim adjustment, will continue to increase as the moving public becomes still more sophisticated. The competition for such an affluent group will require highly professional performance from every employee each day from now on.

Let us consider an average household's move, keeping in mind the above profile of what this average household is like, in terms of education, income, and general sophistication:

John Smith comes home from his commuting train one night in May and announces to his wife that he is being transferred from the New York area where the Smiths now live to a midwestern community of one million population. After her recovery from only mild shock (Mrs. Smith has been used to mobility, for she has moved three times in the last five years as her husband worked his way up the corporate ladder as a salesman for a national magazine), the Smiths then called three moving companies in the suburban Connecticut town that they live in. Although many companies operate otherwise, Mr. Smith's company has asked him to get three independent estimates and report his findings to the company. Bill Jones came out to see Mrs. Smith and to give her an estimate of the total cost of the approaching move. In the process of the estimate, Bill explained some of the industry's problems with estimating: some people don't care how much the move costs if the corporation for which the head of household works is paying the bill. Other people with housing allowances try to sell a good deal of their old or unused furniture, planning to buy new things at the destination city. This kind of activity often makes for differences in the estimate versus the actual cost, Bill explained, for the Smiths might not be able to sell all that furniture as they hoped, and the weight of the actual move would be far above the estimated goal.

Also, as the Smiths were slightly aware, the months of June to September are frantic for the average mover in almost every part of the country. The frenzy is shown by the fact that 44% of all moves made in America occur in those three vacation months, usually in order to coincide with the school recess. Because of the extraordinarily heavy activity of these three months, Bill suggested to Mrs. Smith that she give him at least a month's notice before the actual move took place, so that Bill could meet his plan for moving the Smiths' belongings on the day and even the hour predicted. If Bill was awarded this job, he said, he would hope to pick up the Smiths' household goods some time between the fourth of the month and the twenty-fourth because movers are busiest on the first three days of each month and on the last six days. The Smiths appreciated very much the fact that Bill Jones was open, candid, and completely realistic in his estimate of the cost of the move and in anticipating the problems that the Smiths might encounter. His actual estimate was very much similar to the other two companies selected for submitting estimates, and so his firm was given the assignment. On the day selected for the job, three packers in fresh white uniforms arrived to pack the Smiths' things. They had a motto on their clipboard that was very prominently displayed: "Be a professional in every way." They were. The Smiths' household goods were ready to roll by the end of the day. Bill Jones had stressed that careful handling of fragile items was critical and these men were especially trained in the latest packing techniques to ensure safe transportation of the Smiths' valuables. Also, specially trained men were picked to service electrical appliances in the safest and most efficient way. Meanwhile, school was out, and the Smiths had sold their home. They were to occupy their new home in the Midwestern city to which Mr. Smith had been transferred. A total of ten days, in this specific case, was allotted for the completion of the Smith move. The van carrying their things had other pickups to make along the way. Bill Jones' firm alerted the Smiths 24 hours before the goods were scheduled to arrive. The Smiths were waiting the next morning at their new home with the necessary papers for the driver. In the Smiths' case, Mr. Smith's company was billed for the moving costs. In the "COD" move, the owner of the household goods is usually expected to present a certified check for the amount of the estimate plus 10%. If these charges are higher than the original estimate plus 10%, the household goods are unloaded, but the customer must pay the balance within 15 days, excluding Saturdays, Sundays, and holidays.

The household goods were unloaded in a day's time and everything seemed in good order. The next morning an agent on the unloading end of this journey called Mr. and Mrs. Smith to introduce himself and to explain about a possible claim adjustment if this proved necessary. He also sent along standard claim forms for the Smiths to study after they had inspected the condition of all their household goods. When the Smiths had selected Bill Jones' firm, they decided to take out more than the established 60 cents per pound of coverage that the moving company normally placed on the shipment of household goods. By doing this, they were anticipating "real" value of goods, and not just value based on weight alone. Of course, this is an ideal circumstance, but the Smiths had been fortunate in considering the move from the mover's side of the fence as well as their own. They had considered the problems of proper and accurate scheduling dates, taking into consideration the special seasonal situation that surrounds the moving and storage business. The Smiths were also realistic about the amount of time that the move would *really* take . . . and planned accordingly. On the other end of the line, they were informed of their rights as to claims and to the manner that these claims, should they prove necessary, would be handled. The Smiths found that by open communication, on their part as well as on the part of both the originating agent and the agent at point of destination, there was little if any misunderstanding. . . . In short, the Smiths knew what services they could and should expect.

This kind of active business had not left much time for people working in the industry to record its history. In fact, up to this writing, there had been only a few books published about this important work, and one of them by the acknowledged dean of the industry, Clarence A. Aspinwall, who died in the middle of the 1960's at the age of 89. Mr. Aspinwall's distinguished career had included the presidency and chairmanship of the Security Storage Company of Washington, D.C., where the beginning of this book has deliberately been placed.

In an introduction to the first issue of the National Furniture Warehousemen's Association monthly magazine, *The Furniture Warehouseman,* an industry spokesman, Ralph Wood, secretary of NFWA, apologized for the dearth of material about the business up to that time (November, 1920). Fortunately, this is not the case now. It is possible to form a clear picture today of the industry, but before we can understand the present and the future we must go back to the past. We need to listen to the words of some of the most articulate, involved, and far-seeing gentlemen who have ever had a part in this ubiquitous and vibrant industry.

As one observer of the moving and storage industry pointed out recently: "Aside from the medical profession, there is nothing more 'personal' than the moving business! The doctor pokes and probes the body, and the moving man does almost the same by entering the customer's castle — the home."

2

Beginnings

The immigration was under way. Its great days were just around the turn of Spring—and an April restlessness, a stirring in the blood, a wind from beyond the oak's openings, spoke of the prairies, the great desert, and the Western Sea. The common man fled westward. A thirsty land swallowed him insatiably. There is no comprehending the frenzy of the American folk-migration. God's gadfly had stung us mad.

This haunting and effective description of what makes Americans so constantly in churning movement comes from Bernard De Voto's *Mark Twain's America*. It is as true a statement today as it was when De Voto wrote his book, and was especially true in the times of Mark Twain himself.

However, the process started more than 250 centuries ago when man learned to carry a club to defend himself, and this led to hunting which led to going farther from home and to changing caves from time to time. And when he acquired several clubs and other things, he had to move them. Is it really much different today?

Man is still moving, and rather than using his beasts of burden or his wife to carry his household goods, he is using a moving company; that is, he discovered this after a good many years. Before this discovery, he used his mules, until he became

16

a completely agricultural individual. Then, he simply became bigger in household and possibly more organized—though there is skepticism about this.

When the East Coast became too crowded for the more rugged of our forefathers, these people went West, as Twain's people did, and we had the great trail movements of the nineteenth century, when wagons stuck in the mud so thick that years later the traces could still be clearly distinguished by scholars with the patience to look for them—on the Santa Fe Trail at Fort Union, New Mexico, for example.

Every pioneer family had some kind of cart or wagon in which to make this long, dangerous trek over the mountains and plains to greener pastures in the West—sometimes finding death and horrible torture at the hands of enemies, both human and animal, before the final resting place was found. Fortunately, people persisted; that is why we are here today.

This kind of family travel led to a formation of the first organized mover, rightly called the father of all American moving firms, Pomeroy and Company, which operated along the Eastern Seaboard before the Revolutionary War. Their operations, however, did not extend as far inland as did another well-known establishment, the Wells Fargo Company.

Aside from these few organized companies, the major mover of household goods was the individual American family, with its covered wagon. It was a versatile device that served as a land vehicle, as a home when the night and the fear of the prairie descended on everyone, as a boat when deep streams and rivers had to be crossed—and last of all—as a fort turned on its side or standing straight up when Indians came upon the caravan.

The household goods mover of the past might well have been a wagon master who would go around and organize a dozen families and convince them to set out for better things farther west, with *him* as the leader. Of course, he got paid for it—and he earned every cent of his salary. One of the best descriptions of this kind of man is to be found in A. B. Guthrie's classic

American novel, *The Way West,* which describes in chilling detail what horrors were to be found in a journey through the wilderness. Gradually things became a little more civilized, a little more comfortable, and by the turn of the century the cowboy—and the outlaw—both had to look for new professions.

Of course, of great importance in the late nineteenth century was the role of the railroad. Rail shipments involved cartage by horse-drawn vehicles to a warehouse, where the goods were packed and crated. They were then transported to a rail or water terminal where the goods were arranged to be shipped to point of destination. Upon their arrival, the goods were handled by a corresponding warehouseman at point of destination for uncrating and unpacking and eventual carting to the residence of the customer. The importance of the railroad cannot be underemphasized, but its total involvement is important principally as a forerunner of the moving and storage industry which we are familiar with today, and which is the basic subject for this book.

By 1900 a local company was almost always family-owned, probably a father and son operation, specializing in draying and keeping a livery stable catering to people moving from one dusty street in America to another, and occasionally to another town.

Even in the 1920's a trip by van from one city to another was quite an adventure and a costly one, for more often than not the return trip was made with an empty truck. This point, in the opinion of many experts, is still the critical question of the moving industry: the return load problem and its total cost to everyone involved in the overall moving transaction.

By 1941, when the Fateful Sunday that "will live in infamy" had so changed the lives of all citizens, the moving industry was so well-established that it was never to go backward, except for an interim period in the critical World War II years when shortaged vehicles, tires, and fuel made it necessary to revert to rail movement to handle the really long-distance move. In those hectic days, millions of people picked up their belongings, left families and ties behind, and went to where the jobs were.

By the time of Pearl Harbor, the major national movers were organized, and the roads were reasonably good and uncrowded. If you've ever seen a photograph of a highway in the Pacific Northwest, you can see how relatively alone a motor traveler could still be in America in the early 1940's. Many factors were to change this situation, however.

After the end of World War II, the countless moving of households, factories, and office buildings went on unabated. In fact, more families have probably moved in each year within the United States since the end of World War II than moved in the entire history of the world from the time of Moses to the beginning of the twentieth century.

Of course, behind mass movements you always have people who make up the moves, and those who make them possible. Who were the people who shaped and have continued to shape the philosophy of this dynamic industry?

Fortunately, some of their thoughts are on tape and have been edited for the purposes of this book. As in any endeavor like this, there will be repetitiousness, for these men were in the same business at the same time, competing with others just as intelligent as they were. However, their personal observations are of great interest to any history of this business.

These titans of the industry have been joined by many others who can attest to the way things really were in those bygone days. Above all, this was one of the first and foremost personal businesses — and it still is. For example, at the turn of the twentieth century some independent businessmen in the moving and storage industry thought nothing of going around every morning to a busy corner of their city where they simply "called" for jobs. They took furniture carts and stood waiting for local residents who wished to move their belongings from place to place.

These early businessmen — many of whom would later in life take charge of big, powerful companies — were mainly concerned with local moving. From time to time, these operators did box materials or personal effects to be sent by rail to other parts of the country beyond their usual jurisdiction or interest.

As the automobile and the motor van became a reality and not just a dream of crotchety geniuses like Henry Ford, it was natural that the moving of furniture could be carried on over greater distances from the home base of operations. Although long-distance motor-van moves were rare, they eliminated the cost and the trouble of old-fashioned crating, plus the bothersome rail loading and unloading of goods at departure and destination.

An important development of these times was that warehousemen were linked to each other through the need to have correspondents at rail delivery points, in order to deliver the goods to the shipper's residence. This connection required responsibility for service to the originating warehouseman.

It is safe to say that a pivotal point was reached primarily in the middle 1920's with the advent of reasonably good roads that were being built in all parts of the country. Add to that the advances made technically to motor transportation and you have a growing business volume, one far surpassing even the most imaginative "morning caller" who thought he was on top of his daily challenges. Soon after this need for responsible correspondents became so evident, an equal need for trade associations became necessary to serve these warehousemen at both the origin and the destination of a move, in order to provide the service that was needed for the customer. Not everyone at the beginning recognized this need so clearly, however. Many of these associations were formed originally to deal with ethical questions and concerns in the *warehousing* and not in long-distance moving areas. It is a matter of record that a 1922 report of a conference of Eastern warehousemen on long-distance moving shows that many participants questioned the need for any national long-distance van lines at all. These participants felt that long-distance operations could still be effectively handled by the rail method.

Soon, however, the emergence of national van lines became a vital and sometimes a disturbing force. It took no crystal ball for hard-headed businessmen to see that the lack of return loads for their intercity vans was definitely hurting business. They felt that they were not capitalizing on business that should be there and on the efficient utilization of equipment that was both expensive and heavy. So, these people tried to secure such re-turn loads as they could by forming cooperative return-load ventures.

One of the principal actions of the National Furniture Ware-housemen's Association at this time was the organization of the Inter-City Removals Bureau. An important outgrowth of this activity was Allied Van Lines. Allied's effects up to this day on the industry are so far-reaching that they will appear through-out this narrative.

Another development was the formation of Return Loads Service, Inc., which was organized in 1928, and which was directly responsible for establishing United Van Lines, Inc. In this instance, certificate-holding members in the organization were allowed to register intercity shipments for possible use by other members who were also looking for return loads.

These cooperative agreements were meant to increase reve-nue, not to supplant or to decrease existing long-distance loads. An empty truck anywhere beyond 100 miles then and now indicated a big business headache.

One of the most memorable developments in the eyes of many industry observers was the formation of a firm that had a decidedly different character about it from the start. It has maintained this identity ever since. Unlike some of the other leaders in the field, Aero-Mayflower set out in 1927 *to be a national long-distance mover.* Mayflower set up many sales offices throughout the nation. Unlike the other major organiza-tions, Mayflower was establishing a national organization under ownership capable of producing orders from one end of the country to the other. Variations took place; exclusive franchises had been granted in certain cities to existing warehousemen in order to provide broader coverage with less capital outlay. This closely held Mayflower ownership exists to the present day.

Every business in America has had its share of bloody noses. An early account of the way things *really were* in the moving business could make another book. The sophisticated conditions under which meetings and conventions are held today in the courtly atmosphere of palm-shrouded Boca Raton, for instance, are far cries from the sawdust-covered saloons of Chicago where some early meetings were held.

Daily activities in those early times, in the 1910's and into the 1920's, could get pretty rough. One reporter, Horace Prosser of the St. Louis *Post-Dispatch,* has this to say about one morning's work in the moving business: "A couple of moving companies would show up for a move on a given day and the decision as to who would get the business went to the company with the strongest men. It was not unusual for rivals to grab the same table and pull the legs off of it in a tussle for possession."

Clarence Aspinwall, in writing *The NFWA History in Review,* points out that it was common practice for sharp operators to quote a rate substantially lower than the one they would charge when the furniture was delivered, a habit that is human, perhaps, but far from practical as far as *repeat business* is concerned.

Today's sophisticated moving executive realizes that these events took place; he is aware of the fact that under tough competition deliberate misestimating happens from time to time. However, there are controls now, tariffs, and many think even an overregulated economy with too much control emanating from Washington. These conditions have been undoubtedly subtle outgrowths of forces that are almost overwhelming in their proportions, when one thinks of the growth and the increase in complexity that our economy has seen.

Clarence Aspinwall is on record as saying: "The 1920's was a decade in which the industry was growing rapidly and profits were increasing, a decade for overexpansion, perhaps. In the

1920's the motor truck came into its own. Dirt roads everywhere gave place to paved highways. The horses and the slow-moving electric trucks were abandoned. Household removals to another city were no longer accomplished by crating and shipping by rail, but by loading into a long-distance moving van. Hence, the interchange of shipments between members and problems of packing and shipping were transferred to questions of motor haulage and return loads. . . . An accounting manual was produced; a booklet on household packing and shipping specifications, a booklet explaining and interpreting the Warehouse Receipt Act; Correspondent Shipping Rules; the National Furniture Warehousemen's Association Auto Policy, and the Procedure for Arbitration. Of great interest was the dissemination of information regarding a warehouseman's liability and a proper method for limiting it, along with information regarding fumigation and various sidelines which had been tried out by various members."

The industry was growing up, becoming more formal and experiencing growth and the infusion of new talent from many areas. For example, Mr. Chester A. Nelson, who had at one time been sheriff of that famous resting place for other sheriffs, Tombstone, Arizona, decided to go farther west. He, in fact, purchased the small transfer company that moved his baggage trunks from the railroad station to his first place of residence in Los Angeles. It was in 1918 that Mr. Nelson formed what was later to become Lyon Van Lines. He made the first trip by solid-tire truck between Los Angeles and San Francisco, camping along dirt roads beside the truck at nights. It took six days at that time to make the trip between the two cities.

All businesses are made up of people, and fortunately prominent business leaders in the moving and storage industry have put down their own intimate thoughts, predictions, and occasional regrets for others to learn from. One is Mr. Barrett Gilbert of New York City: "In the early days, before any interstate moves, we concentrated on summer storage — in fact, the big part of the business was summer storage. Many of our customers would put their household goods in storage in early summer and then take them out in the fall. We had as many as thirty to forty customers a day after the first of June. This group, very frankly, came from the laboring classes; this was the way they did their business. To show how times have changed, here are some typical figures from the era: a usual work receipt was for about 300 cubic feet of furniture from a walk-up, cold-water, New York flat. Usually, the dwelling was three or four floors above the street.

"On this kind of job, $10 an hour was the usual fee for a van and four men. The men were paid $38 per week for a driver and $39 a week for packers. A six- or seven-room New York apartment usually took about eight hours to move—at a time when men worked much more than a normal eight-hour day."

"Like many others," Mr. Gilbert said, "we did big business in September and late fall. That was because of the New York landlords, who made it a practice of closing most leases on October 1 of each year. Some business carried over, as a matter of course, into November when redecoration or something special was necessary.

In 1920 Mr. Gilbert went from New York to Washington, D.C., to see the Big Four Transfer Company, and he discussed with F. D. Anderson the setting up of moves between the two cities. Gilbert also stopped in Philadelphia and Baltimore to arrange for moves or partial loads to three cities as a way of increasing his intercity business. At that time, this was called a pool van operation. In 1921 Gilbert made the grand sum of $729 from such an operation, but by 1924 his company was making about $5,000 from the same kind of business, which shows how much things had picked up at that pivotal time in our nation's transportation system. Mr. Anderson followed the first pool trip by rail, stopping at all the cities where they were either picking up or unloading.

Gilbert offers a vigorous description of those days: "In 1924, Boston was also added to the list of cities. An intercity committee of the NFWA, with Martin Kennelly as Chairman, was established to handle some difficult problems. The most sticky was that many members didn't want to surrender their loads to other firms. It was more than just a dollars and cents consideration. It was also the human ego asserting itself. When a man had successfully gained a move, he did not want to put the goods in a truck with another man's name on it.

"From an accounting standpoint, there was really no accurate way of measuring the cubic footage of a load, and on many occasions one mover might say that a particular load made up 500 cubic feet when it was actually much greater. So, the mover hauling a shipment surrendered by another mover could get paid for only the stated 500-cubic-foot price, when in reality it was much more. This was probably the hardest thing for any businessman to take, and such double dealings caused very hard feelings for years afterwards. In fact, such breaches of confidence, when they occasionally occurred, took place the most during the years of 1924 to 1927. An even more bothersome point to the profit-minded entrepreneurs: they were running only about 20% full on return loads, on the average."

Gilbert believed that the National Furniture Warehousemen's Association did offer many critical services in the 1920's, but the exchange of ideas was especially important.

"In those early days, new members could get access to the ideas, methods, and experience of the older warehousemen, the professionals who had been in the business long enough to know what they could do profitably. In general, both the new and the old members gained from bouncing ideas off each other, in correspondence, through the Association magazine, and especially at their conventions."

Charles Morris, Mr. Gilbert felt, was especially effective as the first president of the NFWA. He was articulate, and though he was from New York, which cannot accurately be described as a reflection of the "real" America, he had a sense of national purpose and believed in healthy competition between the Midwest, West, and all areas of the country.

Gilbert's first association in New York was at the Harlem

Storage Warehouse Company in 1890. This was at 211 East 100th Street; in 1906 the name was changed to the Gilbert Storage Company, and in 1945 the Company bought the Bowling Green Storage Company, a firm specializing in overseas work, using the steel lift vans and other heavy equipment current at the time.

Gilbert reports the preponderance of the family flavor to the warehouse business in those early days. There was no labor shortage then, and people tried to pay fair wages. He does see clearly, however, the importance, since that time, of attracting new blood from outside the family to help a growing, demanding, and much more sophisticated clientele. The problem is still to attract someone who will put in as much time as Gilbert and his contemporaries did, in order to build a business. Life styles, to state a truism, have changed.

Anyone familiar with the moving and storage industry could reel off family names and family businesses that come easily to the mind. Just at random, however, the following example shows the ambivalence of this family-dominated business. On one level there is the closeness, the rapport, the feel that a son may have for his father's business. On a completely different basis, there can be a restrictiveness, a lack of outside money and ideas that can result from a purely family-dominated business. The following example is just one of many that could be picked.

Not many people are still around who can remember Herbert C. Neal's grandfather, Jonathan, when he established a drayage firm in Cleveland, Ohio over a hundred years ago. After about ten years in this country as an immigrant from England, J. Neal Moving (and his horse and wagon) became the forerunner of more than 25 vans now being operated by Neal Moving and Storage Company of Cleveland. The Company has proudly moved and stored the household possessions of more than 100,000 families since Jonathan Neal began his business. Herbert C. Neal, today's chief executive, is a photography buff, and when he gets out the old prints there is a definite story that unfolds, graphically telling the role of this family in its own particular industry. Neal's father, Clarence, and his uncle, Arthur, incorporated the firm as Neal Fireproof Storage Company in 1912, and the firm's sales story clearly placed emphasis on the benefits of storing in a concrete building, rather than in the common wooden structures of the day.

Particularly interesting is the appearance of the name Neal everywhere in the tintypes, in the advertising copy, in the efforts to sell the good citizens of Cleveland on the advantages of a family-based, locally operated firm. Herbert Neal has some spectacular photos of what his forefathers were able to do along the line. In 1904, for instance, Neal's grandfather was able to haul and install a 200-ton monument in a cemetery. An equally complicated task was performed in the 1960's when the firm was able to move 44,000 inventors' items, ranging from small, electronic components to a 1-ton valve, in just 11 days. Many families who are moving continue to depend on the firm to do the possible and sometimes the impossible with their latest skills. The Neals now have three facilities in Cleveland.

One family-dominated firm that exercised enormous influence on the early days of the industry, and continues to do so, is the Bekins Moving and Storage Company, and few men are as well-qualified to speak of the history of the industry as Milo Bekins, Sr., an exceptionally energetic man with white hair, a quick step, and a yen still to play tennis daily.

For this book, Mr. Bekins taped some recollections and at a later point wrote the author a long memorandum about his thoughts and feelings about the past, present, and future of an activity that has totally occupied the family since 1895.

"One important situation marked our early days on the West Coast, where operating procedures were so different from those on the East Coast. We *didn't* have the seasonal problems that our associates had in New York, for example. We had really no large apartments or apartment complexes and no traditional closing rushes for rents, as with the October 1 deadline that made life so difficult for those firms working within the confines of Manhattan Island.

"By early 1920 we did away with horses completely and had

semi-trailers that were 20 to 24 feet long. This was a long way from our beginnings in the West when we used two horses to pull the country van. The rig was very light weight and our range was about 40 to 50 miles.

"Also by 1920, we had developed fireproof warehouses. In fact, as early as 1905 Bekins had built a fireproof warehouse in Los Angeles and in 1906 we were building one in San Francisco — when the earthquake hit. The concrete warehouse withstood the quake and we had one of the two motor trucks active in the city at that time. I spent 16 hours a day hauling passengers from the wharf to town for several weeks. . . ."

For someone who can still remember his father going to the office as a matter of routine every Saturday during the 1930's, some of the costs and working conditions that Mr. Bekins describes are most interesting as far as they reflect on this industry and on the changes in American life as well, particularly in terms of prices and wages.

"Packing in those early days was done on a time and material basis, and an early run from Los Angeles to San Diego would cost around $75.00. There was no labor shortage, but our big problem was to establish a rate that was profitable. In 1919, a weight basis was set up and the average cost of a move of about six rooms of household goods from Los Angeles to San Francisco would be about $120.00. There were no minimum rates on trips from Los Angeles to San Francisco because there was a scheduled run. On other runs, to other places, we would have to have a 3,000-pound minimum. In 1920, wages for a nine-hour day, 54 hours a week, were about $40.00 for a driver and $32.00 to $35.00 per week for the helper."

Early interest in the NFWA, of course, was an important part of the Milo Bekins' business philosophy. He had some insight into what could make the business really successful and he thought it lay with establishing trust with the customer, for all the mover had to sell was his personal talent, his ability to serve and satisfy. The establishment of a client-professional relationship, similar to that of a lawyer to his client or a doctor to his patient, was especially necessary. Again and again, this image of the client and the professional who serves him comes up in countless interviews in every part of the country.

In 1922, Bekins was on an NFWA committee, chaired by Walter Sweeting, that recommended the hiring of a Public Relation Agency for the moving industry. Their endeavors did not meet with instant approval or support by the other NFWA members. The Public Relations Committee wanted to create standards for the industry through a supported public relations and advertising program. Even though these programs were not always supported unanimously, other ideas were being adopted.

Warehousemen were instructed on public liability, for instance, and uniform rules that would help both the warehousemen and their customers were set up. In another endeavor, Bekins was able to get the association members interested once more in an organized budgeted program for advertising. He suggested that 4% of gross profits should be devoted each year to such activities. This figure came out of a detailed study that Bekins prepared and submitted to the Association. By today's "consumerism" standards, the figure seems excessively modest, but it was a real breakthrough for that period.

Perhaps some of Milo Bekins' thinking did take hold, for the Association did hire a public relations firm after World War II in order to persuade the general public to use storage, in keeping with its prewar habits; admittedly the War's after effects had changed almost everyone's life style.

Mr. Bekins has said very strongly that there was a definite reason for the establishment of the National Furniture Warehousemen's Association at that time. First of all, too many events were happening too rapidly in the industry; and secondly, the American Warehousemen's Association was already divided into three parts, with the household goods group being the smallest — and receiving very little recognition as the years went by.

Several months later, Floyd Bateman made a trip to the West

Coast to ask the Pacific Coast warehousemen to join NFWA. Bateman was a driving force in starting NFWA, and was in fact its second president. Mr. Bekins remembers Bateman's trip as being quite effective and the Pacific Coast group joined their Eastern and Midwestern associates to form the NFWA. There was a good deal of bitterness on the part of the American group and some NFWA members also held their membership in the American Warehousemen's Association.

Returning to his personal recollections, Bekins did make a very important point that seems to distinguish his firm's history from many others. On the West Coast, his company did not have the bulk of the return-load problem that affected the East because the ratio of loads going from East to West was ten times greater than loads going from West to East. It was not until the mid-thirties that this changed at all. For those West to East moves, Bekins did discover that his firm could ship household goods by water through the Panama Canal, the trip taking perhaps 12 to 14 days from Los Angeles to New York at a much lower rate than by rail. Also, no matter what one might say about California today, with its huge population and other associated problems, the state had one of the best early road programs in the country, making for safe and efficient truck transportation, with a minimum of stall outs and costly delays. Bekins ran a profitable moving operation up and down the Pacific Coast due to these roads and the good California weather.

His experience was similar to many others relating to cubic foot figuring of loads. Soon, a straight weight basis was used and everyone was better served by this method. The Western movers published a list where official scales could be found in every major town along the coast and this worked out well for everyone and made for less hard feelings and inaccuracies.

Mr. Bekins has said in his summary of those days: "We were one of the first companies in the West to have multilocated warehouses, again helped along by the excellent Pacific Coast highways. The electric truck was used for inner-city moves (and certainly could come back in smog-shrouded Los Angeles County). Our family business was one of the first to start pool cars with the railroads sending the furniture along after it had been crated and Bekins started to use lift vans as early as 1920, either by rail or boat."

Overall, Mr. Bekins feels that the code of ethics of both the national and local movers organizations has been the most significant contribution that could be made to the moving industry.

Speaking about ethics, he has a most penetrating point to make about the special relationship of government policy to the railroads and the moving industry. A special low rate for moving was set up, using rail cars, to encourage people to move West. It was called the Emigrant Moving Rate and it stipulated that a full railroad carload of household goods and agricultural equipment could be moved at this much lower rate to the western area. One enterprising company became very prosperous through the use of a plow. They would book many separate shipments in Chicago, load the freight car with this furniture, put in the special plow and ship the entire lot as Emigrant Movables to Los Angeles or San Francisco at markedly reduced rates. These savings caused by these reduced rates were shared between the shipper and the mover. The plow became famous and made more trips across the country than a traveling salesman.

The cliché about man not living by bread alone is certainly true, but the fact that everyone has to eat is just as true in these inflationary times. Speaking to that point, Bekins comments: "It is imperative that owners in the moving and storage business give their employees a share of the profits in the particular company they are working for. The Bekins Company has paid a profit-sharing plan every year for all years except for two during the Depression of the 1930's. I also feel that a stock plan is important for morale and for teamwork. If one does these things with enthusiasm and sincerity, many labor problems will be solved before they have a chance to start."

Recollections of moving executives on the East Coast were

just as vivid as Bekins' were. For example, if you knew Far Rockaway, New York, almost 60 years ago, you knew something of the lost primitive beauty of America, one of the lonely wild beaches that haunted poets and lovers alike fleeing the beginning urban sprawl of Manhattan. One employee of a trucking firm interviewed on a hot smoggy day in New York City's canyons looked back wistfully to the days when he drove his father's horse and wagon to Long Island three or four times a week, settling back about midnight behind the loyal beast and peacefully going to sleep. At dawn, he would awake to find himself on the beach at Far Rockaway, his faithful horse having been on a sort of autopilot during the middle of the night before depositing his master and someone's household goods safely at their destination. The tales of a lost Manhattan, when it made sense to live there, can be found on the lips of many a New Yorker.

One who has prospered here is George Winkler, of John Winkler and Son, Far Rockaway, Long Island, New York. Winkler's first experience in the moving and storage business was as a very young boy with the family firm around 1915. George Winkler was one of the few moving and storage men who went through Notre Dame to graduate in the bleak year of 1930, an accomplishment in itself. The company used horses when Winkler was a small boy, then quickly moved into motor vans when they became available. As he points out, this movement to mechanized transport hardly made the job free of care for either the driver or his helper. There were none of the mechanical devices that we take for granted today, and he worked very long hours. They used to ship by rail, after crating goods, and lift vans were one of the first innovations that he can remember.

After Winkler's graduation, his father encouraged him to develop a specialty that would set their company off from their competitors. The special Winkler technique was rug cleaning, in a time when a prized family rug might have meant as much as Aunt Tilly's jewels. The Winklers prospered at this endeavor, and the opportunity to learn the business from the ground floor gave Winkler a good background for Association work, which he quickly took an interest in.

In fact, in 1954 he became President of the NFWA and before that, as Vice-President, he developed various insurance plans, as well as group plans, retirement and pension plans, and a form of daily coverage that eventually became the Warehousemen's Master Policy. He feels that the movers accomplished all these plans mainly by talking to the right people, the insurance specialists who could do the best job.

Other developments that are prominent in Winkler's memory: Establishment of the Technical Foundation, an important research and education arm of the NFWA; the passing of Public Law 245, which brought household goods from the government warehouse into private warehouses, changing the complexion of the entire industry after World War II and giving servicemen top-rated attention. This development, in Winkler's opinion, put his colleagues back full force into the warehouse business. In this case, an effective lobby was set up. NFWA members went to every Washington hearing on the bill and persuaded their members to write to their senators and congressmen. NFWA presented facts that proved that private industry could do the job at a lesser cost than the government could.

NFWA demonstrated on this occasion that it best represented the warehousing industry and the people who worked in it. In fact, members simply showed that with proper insurance and control they could run the neatest ship in the industry, in Winkler's opinion. Very important in this was Ed Byrnes, the then executive director, a man with a sense of responsibility, the ability to make a decision—and the objectivity to laugh once in a while when the going got especially heavy.

Much could be written about Ed Byrnes' contribution in a number of areas of the moving and storage business. At a testimonial dinner given for him in Chicago, Byrnes was cited for his strong leadership as executive secretary of the NFWA during some of the toughest battles with the federal government.

He was particularly effective in his efforts to help more than just the large operators in the business. He was aware of and constantly interested in helping the small mover as well.

Pallet warehousing came in during the middle forties and Mr. Winkler thinks that this made a big change in the industry. One of the leaders in the building changes that took place at this time, when the pallet warehouse was trying to prove itself, was Herb Holt, manager of Bekins' Los Angeles office, who was a vigorous advocate of the one-story warehouse and the effective utilization of space in each warehouse. Several warehouses built around the country during the 1940's and the 1950's reflect this vision, and many warehouse owners could see the wisdom of this plan when they saw their profit margins rising.

Winkler sees the future as enormously promising. He sees more use of rail moving with piggyback, when dispatching and claim problems can be ironed out. He sees the reemergence of electric trucks for city use, as many others do, because of the public's fierce desire for clean air, especially if these electric trucks could have the speed of gasoline-powered vehicles.

Winkler feels that the problems of the multistoried warehouse that are so common in the metropolitan areas throughout the country are still not solved, and more basic research is needed on this problem. The overriding consideration, he thinks, is that the young men coming into the business will not accept tried and true methods as easily as before; the young will experiment.

Frank Payne, Sr., and his son, Frank, Jr., were honored recently as the first father and son ever to serve as presidents of the NFWA. Frank, Sr., started in the business in 1922 — just at the time that the motor truck took over, from the horse and wagon, to set the standards that are being followed to this day. He was something special in those days; he was a college graduate and grew to be so proficient at his job and at industry functions, where various assignments were handed him, that he became President of NFWA in 1942–1943.

Lyon Van Lines has always occupied a special situation because of its Western location and its history reflects the changes of the industry since 1920.

Although things got rough for Lyon and for most other moving and storage firms in the Depression, the bottom never dropped out. People were moving in with friends and relatives, combining the best of both families' furniture and putting the remaining amount in storage. Late in the 1930's, as the Japanese buildup in military power became alarmingly evident to sensitive observers located on the West Coast, Lyon was called in to do more and more military work for United States government installations up and down the Pacific coastline.

In 1941, for instance, the company moved equipment for the government from Riverside, California, to San Francisco, to replace all the equipment that was lost in the devastating attack at Pearl Harbor. But even before our entry into the war was finally made clear by the Japanese attack, Lyon was moving airplanes and airplane parts and the company was probably as active as any mover in the military involvement of the country from 1941 to 1945.

Because of their location, Lyon has stored film for Hollywood producers and watched over the fantastic growth of West Coast life since the company first started to open *branches* on July 1, 1928. Many things stick in Payne's memory: the early conventions where ideas were exchanged well into the night, where the lack of official written communication might well be solved by an all-night bull session, where philosophy was transferred into hard news for decisive action the next day.

Like so many industry leaders, Frank Payne, Sr., feels that the National Furniture Warehousemen's Association has succeeded beyond the wildest dreams of what could be called a simply organized dream for universal cooperation from coast to coast. He thinks that containers, by rail, will come back into their own, so that operations from crating and shipping by rail with motor van in direct involvement will again be popular, when the problems of container specifications and interstate and interregulatory body warfare can be reduced for the good of all. Since Lyon went on its own, after the break with Allied Van Lines, Inc., in the middle 1940's, Lyon has had a unique position in the industry.

Mr. Payne feels that for future growth of the NFWA, the Association must attract more members and it must increase its educational thrust, holding more of those valuable seminars which he has found so helpful. His thoughts bear repeating and have been considered carefully in all parts of the country, besides the West.

One crucial area in this industry has been and will probably always be the Midwest. A meeting in Chicago with Arthur Reebie, President, Reebie Storage and Moving Company, can convince anyone of the continuing power of job enthusiasm to keep a man young at heart, no matter what his age.

Hearty, husky, and acute, Reebie was in his 81st year during the time of this interview and the firm was in its 91st year. The conversation ranged over a number of topics. He talked about the many times his father went out to buy horses and sold them around the near northside, the time his father *bought* a circus because it was going bankrupt. This showed young Arthur that he could stay home and enjoy the world while his friends had to run away. After all, he owned his own circus.

About business, Reebie had this to say: "Most of the established moving and storage companies started out with a horse, a wagon, a determined individual—*and a strong back.* . . . Some progressed; others that did not keep up with the requirements of the industry fell by the wayside. . . . There have been great changes in the Chicago area—ethnic changes and great moving patterns from family homes to high-rise apartments. There has been a great exodus to the suburban areas for families with children; there was a general need to better the environment. . . . A considerable amount of our business in the suburban areas results from the transfer of executives of large corporations. Some of these corporate transfers take people to other areas of the country and an increasing amount to foreign

countries. . . . I think the future possibilities of the moving
and storage business are good. Storage business in the city of
Chicago tends to be the smaller-type lot, whereas the storage
business in the suburban areas is usually of larger households.
Overhead and labor costs are constantly rising, as in all businesses today. Some of the sons of the older established firms
stay in the business but many have tried other fields . . . with
more opportunity."

Reebie's position in the newly opened suburban area of Chicago, as North Clark Street was some years ago, made him an
important observer of the industry in this centrally located
industrial town. His war record and his ability to survive crises
of all kinds make him an exceptional observer of the business.

Reebie was a fine scholar, graduating from the University of
Michigan in 1912, whereafter he immediately went into the
sales branch of the business, spending several illuminating
years putting into effect the theories that he was taught in Ann
Arbor.

After a stint in the Mexican War of 1916, Reebie found himself back at the family business where he began working in
estimating. Growth patterns at the time were especially interesting in Chicago, for near northside activity and the movement
of affluent northside families to that area was much similar to
what was happening in other parts of the country. In New York,
for instance, everyone was going north of 42d Street to upper
Park Avenue and upper Fifth Avenue.

It was a volatile time in America and in the world too, for
Arthur was again recalled to service, this time to found a moving business in the south of France with the American Expedi-
tionary Forces. He soon learned that many of the people he
recruited to work in the transportation corps would later become some of his best friends and competitors in Chicago's
world of moving and storage leaders.

The stakes after World War I were high. Reebie's father had
agreed shortly after the close of the war to build a new building
that would cost the gigantic sum of from $250,000 to $300,000.

The Reebies raised the capital somehow, and when their imaginative Egyptian-style building was put up they found it half full with storage the first year.

The Reebies have not been unlike others—they did everything in those days they could to survive. They bought coal and wood and sold it on the streets in winter. They sold beer or their trucks hired out for that purpose, when the months got hot. They bought and sold horses; they made the business go.

In the south of France during the First World War, Arthur Reebie knew what it was like to see sons die. In his own family he has seen the same thing. Theirs is a proud history and Reebie has carried on the prosperous business from their unusual building, standing out so distinctly now amid the jumble of northside Chicago.

As Reebie said recently, he first met Milo Bekins, Sr., in California in 1903. Both are still active, and perhaps it is their vital interest and participation in their industry that keep them so fit and vigorous today.

Another vigorous and articulate spokesman is C. D. Morgan, of Morgan and Brother Manhattan Storage Company, Inc., of New York City.

"In 1851," Mr. Morgan began, "the time of the dreaded potato famine in Ireland, many new businesses were started in the United States by people from all over Europe, and in our case from Ireland; My grandfather, Patrick Morgan, and his brother, Frank, saw that there was no such thing in the New York area as a true moving van, in the sense that we know them today. My grandfather and my uncle remembered a certain moving company, very informally structured, in Ireland, so the Morgan brothers decided they would start one in the New World.

"They went into the ginger ale business at 47th and Broadway, where the Edison Hotel now stands. Within a few months, Frank Morgan continued with the ginger ale business and my grandfather, Pat, went into the moving business full-time. Both my grandfather and my uncle shared a warehouse which they used for various kinds of storage. In our family records, we have, in fact, moving and storage receipts from jobs conducted early in 1851. My father went into the business in 1890 and my brother Arthur and I entered the business about 1920.

"Arthur has just retired and I will also in a few years, because now we are fortunate in having our own sons running the business, just as we took over from a previous generation of Morgans. The active management now includes my sons, Sadler and Artie, and my brother's son, Charles. In any business it is unusual to have four generations that can survive fires, floods, wars, and still flourish."

Morgan has seen great change in the four generations of the family business: "In 1890, my father decided that the family could make a decent living in this business because the competition was not as stiff as it later became. On the other hand, when I started in working for the family firm in about 1920, the competition was much rougher because we had to meet Gilbert, Manhattan Storage, Santini and Chelsea in open street competition. There were also many small firms only beginning in the business. Many of these small companies have grown much stronger and are more prominent today than ever before.

"My generation was particularly noted for formalizing the industry. We started to form associations, we adopted cost accounting schedules, so that we could give more intelligent and comprehensive estimates than had existed before."

One important event before Mr. Morgan's formal entry into the family firm occurred in 1915, when the first union contract for the Morgan organization was signed in a saloon at 47th street and Eighth Avenue in New York by Mr. Morgan's father and uncle. The union was represented by John McKenna, who was a packer at the time for the Budworth Company. The union realized fully that they had to help the industry if their members were to prosper and make a living wage. Because of this understanding between management and labor, the industry is as strong as it is today, in Morgan's opinon.

"There was a feeling of general cooperation in those early

days among competitors that is unique, I think, in American business. For instance, my father's good friends were Grant Wayne, Bill Woods, Charlie Morris, Bill Bostwick, John Neiser, and Louis Schramm, Sr., all of whom were deeply involved in New York moving and storage work. I can remember attending a big parade in Manhattan in Louis Schramm, Sr.'s big car, which was quite a status symbol for a youngster in those days."

Another big development in the labor relations area, in Mr. Morgan's opinion, was the 1932 strike that lasted for seven weeks. Louis Schramm, Jr., Ed Sullivan, and Morgan were all active in trying to settle it, and after those trying times the union and management understood each other better than ever before — even though the process demanded great patience on both sides.

"But in 1937 there was another strike and the Movers and Warehousemen's Association of New York City was formed. This strike was a cooperative effort, as strange as it may sound to some current observers of the labor-management scene, in order to stabilize conditions throughout the industry. For example, in those difficult days, rates could be drastically cut at any time by anyone, in order to get a job no matter how unprofitable it might be. Times were just that tough.

"The industry was in real financial trouble. The warehouse storage rates had gone down: Manhattan Storage, the largest in the city, had established a storage rate of ¾ cents per cubic foot and moving charges were put at a flat rate — so many dollars per room . . . We stabilized the rates at six dollars (per hour) per van and three dollars a man (per hour), for the smaller operator, and seven dollars a van and three dollars a man for the larger companies.

"Cost differentials to help small businessmen get their share of the moving pie came into existence then. Now we have lower tariff rates protecting these small, independent moving companies. I think this was the smartest thing that the industry could have done, especially under the chaotic circumstances that prevailed, and I know of no other industry in American life that has acted accordingly."

Then Mr. Morgan started to discuss another important topic: "I recall the agony of getting an Impartial Chairman in New York to settle all complaints from customers about their claims and the differential that often occurs between estimate and actual, final cost. This man's word, after he had been selected, was to be final in any dispute. It was most difficult to find an arbitrator who was acceptable to all parties in the industry who had to deal with him. This search caused many hard feelings, but the Impartial Chairman's post is still active and successfully operating in the New York area today."

Even a critic of the business world like Ralph Nader agrees with Morgan's statement, and has praised the Impartial Chairman's role in New York in his recent book with the ironic title, *The Interstate Commerce Omission.*

One might say that the moving business really came of age in the 1920's. At the beginning of the decade, in a historic July meeting at Mackinac Island in Michigan, the National Furniture Warehousemen's Association was born. There were 50 printed pages of proceedings arguing the pros and the cons of the organization of such a group. Just as the times were in ferment, so was the association of members which was not yet a full-fledged association of anything or anybody. In a secret ballot 325 attendees to that meeting voted for the Association and 25 voted against. There was one lonely blank ballot.

The NFWA was growing with the new mobility. Moving and storage companies went on multiplying, using family talent, occasionally hiring someone from outside who looked as if he could work long and hard hours.

It was the time that America came out of the country, and the moving business was there to move Americans wherever they wanted to go. This enormous activity made a young industry into a major national force. These leaders cited here were only a few men among many who had the same dream: the exchange of ideas among moving men in every part of the country. Especially important was the movement Westward, to coincide with the general movement of the country's population and business activity.

As these moving and storage men saw the need for greater communication among themselves on a national basis during the 1920's, their sons have seen this need become one of an international kind.

The leaders in this young industry were not afraid to take a chance on the future, to gamble that the years ahead would be good ones. To make the most of these years, they were eager to pull together on a national basis. It wouldn't be long before this optimism was to undergo one of its biggest challenges.

3

Hard Times

A s the troubled decade of the 1930's began, one of the tried and true maxims of the moving and storage industry was put to its stiffest test. Was the industry really "Depression-proof?" The years ahead were to show that the business would survive, but not without enormous difficulties.

These *were* tough years, times to test the strongest of companies as well as those firms that were not so well off financially. Milo Bekins, Sr., comments about his Depression days and how his firm weathered the tough tests of those times:

"As everyone knows, the Depression years of the 1930's were difficult ones. However, we had faith not only in our own business but in the future growth of California— and beginning in 1930 we built a new warehouse on Brand Boulevard in Glendale of about 45,000 square feet. We added 20,000 square feet to our Sacramento warehouse and purchased the business and facilities of the McClintock Storage Company in San Diego, a 60,000-square-foot warehouse. We also bought the City Transfer Company in Long Beach with its seven-story building of 44,000 square feet. In 1932, we purchased the Highland Avenue warehouse of the Hollywood Storage Company, a 13-story building with 156,000 square feet."

As others were retrenching, Bekins was pursuing its earlier dreams by taking some chances. Perhaps the reason for taking these chances was that the Pacific area just didn't see as much chilling poverty and despair as the East and the Midwest. However, it was in California that *The Grapes of Wrath*, the famous John Steinbeck novel, was set about the Oakies and their plight. Of course, this condition didn't apply to everyone.

Mr. Bekins goes on to tell what his firm was doing at the time. "Many companies were having a difficult time in operating at a profit and thus were willing to consider selling their businesses." Quite a few business leaders who survived and even prospered were able to see a way out. Of course, just like the man who invested in real estate at the time, it took a little money to make a little money.

Here is what Milo Bekins has said: "The purchase of the Wilshire Storage Company in 1932 dates back to a time when the Neal Company of Cleveland and the Lyon Company of Los Angeles and our company were contemplating building warehouse buildings in the Wilshire District of Los Angeles in 1932. I suggested it would be unwise for each of us to build and independently operate three warehouse facilities to serve this district and that we should join forces, each of us taking a third interest in a new company known as the Wilshire Company. They built one building in 1924 of 46,000 feet with an addition in 1928. . . . We brought a warehouseman out from Chicago and that worked out successfully. However, in 1929, Clarence Neal desired to dispose of his third interest, which we purchased. The business, however, continued to operate independently until 1932 when it appeared that it was difficult to operate at a profit. Subsequently we bought out the Lyon third interest. . . . I think the results of our expansion during the ten-year period known as the Depression period were extremely satisfactory and a fair accomplishment when one considers that during this period we added a total of 511,000 square feet of warehouse facilities."

Mr. Bekins has some other points to make about the decade that show the enormous change of the times and how they could work to the advantage of some, to the disadvantage of others.

"It was during this Depression period that we expanded our motor lines operations into the East as well as into the Northwest. In 1935, the federal government passed the so-called Motor Carriers' Act. This brought regulations under which the household-goods motor carrier industry must operate."

It was becoming increasingly evident that the federal government was now treating the moving and storage industry as a national force in a mobile society. The regulations and restrictions that were being enforced in other walks of life were not to be ignored when it came to considering how people moved their belongings from one part of the country to another by motor van. As surely as these regulations must have reduced many irregularities in the operation of certain moving and storage companies, making for a fair treatment of the shipper and consumer, these rules and restrictions forced a great deal of compliance and restraint that energetic entrepreneurs found difficult to accept. This degree of acceptance has never been constant from that important year of 1935 to the present time.

Industry leaders had mixed reactions to say the least. Again, here is what Milo Bekins thought about those critical years and the role of the federal government in the operation of the industry: "The federal government brought out many regulations under which the household-goods motor-carrier industry must operate. We held meetings and discussions among the Bekins organizations in California, Bekins-Northwest, Bekins-Omaha-and-Sioux City, and Bekins-Texas (all of whom were, up to this time, operating individually owned companies) with the idea of consolidating our long-distance operations into one Bekins nationwide company. This resulted in the filing of an application before the Interstate Commerce Commission for merging the rights held by all Bekins companies into a nationwide organization which resulted in the incorporation of the Bekins Van Lines Company with operating rights in 45 of the then 48 states. At a later date, rights were purchased in the remaining states—three New England states—so that complete coverage was available."

By taking a bit of a chance, Bekins was ready for the expansion of its operations just before World War II. The overall plan was that the Bekins Van Lines Company would own the semi-trailers and the individual Bekins companies would furnish the tractor service to haul these semi-trailers through to their destination. This type of operation proved very efficient, as did the shuttle system, which provided continual movement of the semi-trailer by the use of drivers living in the western cities where the tractor was kept on a 24-hour hauling service.

Although some companies like Bekins were ready for expansion when the doldrums of the Depression passed, others were diversifying in order to stay competitive and often capitalizing on the times better than they ever had before. For example, the Fidelity Storage and Warehouse Company in Orlando, Florida, started to act as complete caretakers for the homes of wealthy residents who fortunately for them still had large homes to worry about.

One New York retailing tycoon established the pattern in those years of merely dropping off his house key at the warehouse office before heading with his wife for a train to New York City. The warehouse company took up the rugs; put the silverware in a warehouse vault; wrapped all the furniture, mattresses, and pillows; covered the pictures and other art pieces, barred the windows; and closed the house. When the family returned in late fall from their northern home, the house was automatically opened and aired and everything was in order when the executive and his family arrived from the station.

From five to eight men spent approximately two or three days in a single house. In one week, the Fidelity Storage and Warehouse Company closed three homes in this manner. In one case, even a yardman was hired by the week and instructed to inspect the grounds from time to time to see that they were being properly maintained. Again, this kind of attention, supervision, and care could only be carried on in such a time when service made the difference between who worked and who did not. The man who prospered really had to earn his keep.

Perhaps it is only human, perhaps it is peculiarly American, but it is difficult to find today a complete and candid description of the way things really were in these "difficult days." Now that the pain is far behind, people simply don't want to talk about those times.

However, the grim facts of economic life were lightened from time to time by various commentators who wrote about business life. One man whom many remember as a penetrating analyst was H. F. MacNiven, full secretary of the National Furniture Warehousemen's Association, a man possessing wit and insight. He contributed regular editorials to industry journals of those days.

In that dark year of 1931, he had these curiously refreshing comments to make: "There must be something to the predictions that we are heading for better times. I was recently in an eastern state, covering our membership, and I found good storage business and some people very busy with local moving jobs. . . ." In addition to these optimistic remarks, Mr. Mac-Niven supplied the following practical information:

"There were exceptions of course, companies who had pushed merchandise storage and who had, unfortunately, forgotten household goods, and these were naturally hard hit, as merchandise storage in that locality was practically flat. . . . But within the last few months, I have noticed a better and more cheerful attitude almost everywhere I have been, and this is particularly true since March."

Unfortunately, there were to be several years more of this "flatness" before times were really good again. Many distinguished historians have pointed out that Franklin D. Roosevelt had his back against the wall over the economic state of the nation before the Japanese attack on Pearl Harbor. It is no secret that the Second World War bettered economic conditions for civilians, while thousands of fighting men lost their lives. There simply was no answer to the dilemma.

No matter what historians eventually decide about this decade, the effects of the Depression on the moving and storage industry, which is so tied to every form of human activity and movement, were felt to be catastrophic in many cases and in almost every part of the country.

MacNiven had other comments to make about the state of the nation: "On my last trip, I heard much talk regarding the debt moratorium. The executives interviewed seem to feel that if is is adopted, it might help in a psychological way only, but the wage earners seem to have the idea that it means the start of better times, which would tend toward freer buying on their part, and it would remove a considerable amount of the uncertainty which we have all been dealing with. . . . Much is said about developing sideline revenue, and I have found some movers acting as distributors of electric refrigerators, thus securing additional revenue during summer—which is the busiest period of the year for the dealers of mechanical refrigeration."

Indeed, this was not an idle prediction of things to come. It is interesting to speculate on how many firms flourishing today might have been deeply involved in 1931 in furniture sales of repossessed and unclaimed household goods, and the other sidelines of machine distribution and sales that led to life-long occupations. Drapery storage and rug cleaning became profitable sidelines for warehouseman, for instance, all over the country. Many other sidelines were developed, but fear of the future was everywhere. It was a time to adjust or to perish. Some accounts were filled with contradictions.

It was at this time that MacNiven found a warehouseman who was storing refrigerators for three highly competitive firms in the same market. This same man delivered and set up the refrigerator in the home of the customer. Anything strange about this? Of course not. The man's employees had become expert in the installation of this special equipment and this capability left the dealer more time and energy to concentrate on developing additional sales revenue through the sale of *more* refrigerators. Thus, countless businessmen learned to adjust and many an ancillary business was formed, which in some cases became more lucrative than the original one had been in this uncertain Depression economy.

NFWA members often paid close attention to what Mr. Mac-Niven had to say, and his advice was followed to the letter. During one MacNiven trip, for example, a moving man eliminated the words "fireproof storage" from the company title and substituted "fireproof warehouse." The supposedly simple change did wonders for the company image. Also, upon following MacNiven's advice, this same member had so reorganized the usable space in his warehouse by restacking that instead of a warehouse chock full of goods that permitted no new business, the member found that he had one-half of one floor empty for extra business, with enough newly created space for five additional van loads.

And there were exciting moments associated with the business from time to time. That great American tycoon, lover, and mystery man, Howard Hughes, figured in a memorable story during the early part of the decade. It seems that Mr. Hughes, at the time one of the world's greatest and boldest racers of airplanes, had broken the existing record of 314 miles per hour air speed over a 6-mile course by flying 347.29 miles an hour. The 314-mile-per-hour record was set in France several months before.

In the early 1930's, such daring feats as Hughes' had to be officially recorded on sensitive instruments—a chronometer, barograph, chronograph, and two high-speed cameras which recorded images at the rate of $\frac{1}{1000}$ of a second. Official timing of Howard Hughes' historic flight was in the hands of William Inyart of Washington, D.C., secretary of the National Aeronautical Association's contest board. After completion of the flight, Inyart called Bekins Moving and Storage in Los Angeles for the assignment. It was crucial that things be handled correctly.

The extremely sensitive equipment was completely packed and shipped by Bekins to the National Aeronautical Association archives in Washington with no questions asked by the Board.

In many ways, it was a tribute to a still young industry, as the reporter writing the story at the scene pointed out. The move of highly sensitive equipment called attention to the moving and storage industry's increasing prestige. It is very possible that these incidents led to the tremendously profitable work that such leaders as Neptune and other companies have done for International Business Machines, North American Rockwell, and others. Companies who specialize in having mobile, highly sensitive equipment available at a moment's notice can be traced to such early times as these.

One fascinating person who attended the Hughes' flight and then shortly disappeared from the earth completely was Amelia Earhart, the woman aviator about whom so much has been written. Her working for Franklin Roosevelt as a spy against the Japanese is one story that has been widely circulated. As a symbol of the 1930's, she is unique, and she witnessed a first for the moving industry—one that opened as many new horizons as she did in her own airplane.

To most warehousemen, these dramatic special moves were few at the time. Economic conditions of the country made these men look for better ways to operate their businesses and to cut costs as much as possible. An excellent summary by an anonymous editor in *The Furniture Warehouseman* describes a nationwide survey of truck operations conducted by the General Motors Truck Company. The report is a most clear picture of what was going on then, what needed to be done, and what some progressive firms were doing to accomplish these goals. Entitled "Increasing the Mover's Profits with Trucks," the study examined almost every kind of American moving and storage operation—large, middle-sized, and small—in every part of the country. Its major findings were produced by eyewitnesses reporting from the scene. According to Paul W. Feller, then President of the General Motors Truck Company, trained investigators rode thousands of miles on the roads with van drivers, studying operating procedures, checking equipment for its proficiency, and even photographing interesting variations in equipment and operation whenever the occasion presented itself.

The report was divided into the following sections: "Making Moving Day Profits;" "Managing Trucks for Greater Profits;" "Increasing Profits by Better Planning;" "Using Records to Control Trucks;" and "Buying Trucks for Greater Profits."

Candid comments from both leaders and followers in the industry were not long in rolling into the research headquarters. For example, "We make our profit from storage and warehouse functions. *We lose money, frankly, or just break even, on moving!*"

This terse statement was made in the May, 1931, issue of *The Furniture Warehouseman,* when times were bad and going to get worse. Even though it was May, the economic conditions were pretty chilly all over America.

Much of the information contained in this 1931 report remains just as true today as it was then. For instance: "One of the major truck problems encountered by moving and storage companies is the fact that the moving business pays a profit in only 40 to 60 days of the year, in the average community."

Another important recommendation to come out of the survey stated: "To reduce the amount of idle truck time during normally dull periods, based on the feast or famine conditions of the industry—either too much work and not enough people or not enough activity and people sitting around—increase the amount of work, working longer hours, during peak periods, when extra work is reasonably easy to get. Also, reduce waste by cutting staff when things are slow, keeping them in touch for rehiring when the peak period again reasserts itself; but don't cut good drivers."

Getting and keeping competent drivers, so common a complaint today, was always a problem in the early 1930's. This might seem surprising to observers of the industry, considering how fierce competition for jobs was at the time.

"Good drivers mean greater profits from truck operations," said the report. "A sound program for hiring, training and holding the right men pays genuine dividends." . . . In cross-country interviews, under palm trees in Florida or beside the Pacific Ocean in California, one hears the same report today: "Where are the people, and how do we get them?"

However, after the proper people were on the job, the cost factor in those perilous times was extremely important. The report stressed this point. "After the extra time has been saved (from rescheduling during peak periods and winding down during slack ones), then the problem is to make this saving profitable through proper scheduling of loads and by eliminating as much *underloading* as possible either by using some light-duty equipment or by combining small lots."

Some of the suggestions and comments are truistic to any reasonably well-informed businessman, but as indicators of the times they are valuable. One other all-encompassing way to increase profits was suggested by the investigators: hire extra trucks for peak periods and maintain a smaller fleet during normal business pressures. Level off these peaks of activity (which really did hurt efficiency and customer relations) by appealing to the customer himself, explaining the situation and asking him to wait until he could get the full benefit of the professional mover's attention. The same approach was recommended to rental agents and even public utilities.

Cooperative advertising was advanced as another way to increase profits. It was pointed out that this method had produced mixed reactions in every business, and that no real results were available at that time by which to evaluate how well the plan might work.

Another suggestion was to keep trucks busy during dull periods by contracting with concerns which usually are not obliged to make immediate deliveries, or which enjoy a peak season in months when the moving business is slow. Department stores at Christmas might be the best example of this, the report suggested. All seemed simple, solid, and reasonable recommendations that many a warehouseman could put to good use.

Any trained observer could tell that the purpose of such an ambitious research study in this grim time was made to sell more trucks on the part of General Motors. . . . And why not? But another value was obvious. Up to this time, there had been no widespread dissemination of information, except through industry magazines and various conventions, that could apply to all parts of such a huge, largely rural country like America. Its roads were uneven in quality and quantity; its inhabitants moved without notice to all parts of the country, for completely different reasons in New York from those that prevailed for example in Iowa. Many men at all levels of all kinds of companies could now use the report's findings in numerous ways.

An equally helpful summary of the major issues (and their analysis) was published in this same May, 1931, issue of *The Furniture Warehouseman.* Here are some of the conclusions:

"1. Increase work accomplishment by eliminating losses and by better planning of work to be handled by the truck.

"2. Establish rigid control of work accomplishment and costs by setting up and using an effective system of truck records.

"3. Test the suitability and economy of trucks at frequent intervals to guard against losses from equipment which should be replaced.

"4. Buy the truck that is best suited to the job, when new equipment is needed."

It goes without saying that the General Motors Corporation hoped the new trucks to be purchased would be GM trucks.

Of course, life then was a little more complicated than this survey showed. Many people couldn't afford apples on the street corner, let alone buy a truck. However, enough people did prosper so that many problems of growth were presenting themselves to various members of the industry.

One of the men who saw most of this growth take place in the moving and storage industry is David Brodsky, a heavy-browed man who attends to detail with the attention of a fine lawyer, which he is. He came into the business when things were grim, and, ever since his first office as an attorney was opened in New York in the early 1930's, the majority of his work has been for this industry.

He can undoubtedly discuss more cases that directly affected the business than any man alive, and his overview of these important years has been especially valuable in the preparation of this history. His remarks have been considered with special emphasis on the growing and changing years, as they relate to the industry. Brodsky has the singular ability to see history from other peoples' eyes and, therefore, retains that rare quality of objectivity.

As a lawyer, Brodsky has been trained to summarize fast and well. The year 1935 was crucial for the moving and storage industry because of the laws that were being formulated then that would regulate interstate moving. This rock, dropped in the pool of transportation affairs, as it were, has not stopped spreading its long-lasting effects since that year. The effects largely center on the relationship to the public that the industry serves, and on the regulation of the industry by Washington in order to better serve the public. The various divisions of this public are: the private mover (husband and wife), the corporation customer, the military mover (both within the United States and abroad), and the customer who wishes to store his household goods.

One day in early 1934 David Brodsky's partner, the late J. Almyk Lieberman, brought in a clipping from a copy of the *New York Times* concerning the upcoming passage of the Motor Carriers Act, announcing the ICC's jurisdiction over motor carriers. These two young lawyers decided that this was an opportunity too good to pass up, as there were few people who understood the new regulation.

They immediately published a book explaining the new laws and sent a bulletin to movers listed in the Manhattan telephone book. Many responses came back surprisingly quickly. In all, the two young lawyers filed almost 300 applications for "Grandfather Rights." These Grandfather applications laid the basis for the issuance of certificates that are very valuable now.

Brodsky could see that many firms that were filing Grandfather applications without legal help were filing improperly, thereby losing rights which could prove so profitable in the future. A second part of the new law called for the filing of tariffs. Soon, Brodsky held powers of attorney for approximately 250 small movers in the New York City area, and planned on filing tariff rates for these movers as a group.

However, a meeting took place a short time later that Brodsky feels significantly altered the course of events. One morning Louie Schramm, Jr., of the Chelsea warehouse in Manhattan, suddenly appeared in Brodsky's offices. Schramm was one of the big operators in New York. He and his associates in other major firms were very interested in meeting Brodsky face to face and wanted to see what rates he was going to file for these small moving companies. Schramm wished Brodsky to file with a group of movers forming in Washington, D.C.; this group was called the Household Goods Carriers Bureau—a group filing for movers from the entire country.

Brodsky was not favorably disposed to turning his clients over to a group that was controlled from Washington, D.C., and consequently he and Louie Schramm agreed to help organize the Interstate Household Goods Movers Tariff Bureau, now the New York Movers Tariff Bureau, a group with 90% of the New York area movers participating in it. Many of Brodsky's clients were independents and didn't want to have as high a tariff rate as the big companies. A great many refused to go along with the Brodsky-Schramm idea; these movers formed the Independent Movers and Warehousemen's Association (later changing their name to Movers and Warehousemen's Association of America). Their tariff rates have at times been almost 15% lower than those of the larger companies.

The Washington bureau and the New York bureau later made an agreement in which Washington set the long-distance tariff rates and the New York group set their own tariff rates for their immediate areas.

During this time, Brodsky met a man who was to have quite an effect on his professional life. His name was Ed Sullivan.

Sullivan was secretary of the Van Owners Association, which was composed mainly of the larger moving companies in the New York City area. By 1937, the Movers and Warehousemen's Association replaced the Van Owners Association as the Employers Association under contract with the union. Sullivan moved into Brodsky's New York legal offices to continue as a representative of the employers in handling union problems.

Sullivan had a fourth grade education . . . and had learned much of his vast knowledge on the streets of New York. Because he was almost 20 years older than David Brodsky, it took some time for the older man to except the younger. He did though and soon they formed a close bond. Sullivan's basic duty was to work with the union and he had an instinct for telling almost immediately what people he could deal with effectively and with whom he could not. He was rarely wrong.

For example, he kept a list of "good guys and bad guys," to use Brodsky's phrase, that defied logic but still worked. Sullivan believed that a man who could be trusted could *always* be trusted no matter what—and the opposite held true, just as infallibly. Nevertheless, when Sullivan died he left a list of people with Brodsky, detailing the good and bad people based on experience gained in 30 years' negotiating work. He died in the late 1940's, and his last request to Brodsky was that he attend as many funerals as possible of the bad guys which Sullivan was not privileged to witness.

A colorful character making a name for himself in New York was Jimmy O'Neill, who came from England in the early 1930's. He first landed a job as a masseur in a Turkish bath in Manhattan and later became a salesman for one of the commerical movers in New York. From this beginning in the business, he met Charlie Byrnes who owned a warehousing firm in New York. Jimmy made a deal with Byrnes in which each one took a life insurance policy on the other. The estate of the first man to die received the insurance money, while the remaining partner received the entire business. There was one factor that favored O'Neill in this business relationship: Mr. Byrnes drank a good deal and Jimmy had reason to believe that he could out-live him. He did.

Jimmy O'Neill eventually became the owner of Byrnes Brothers. He later bought two smaller warehousing companies, but his real opportunity to become a major operator came along when the Vanderbilt family decided to sell the Lincoln Warehouse at 70th Street and Third Avenue. Jimmy sold everything that he owned and bought out the Lincoln Warehouse. This made him a major operator in the city virtually overnight. He developed an extremely profitable business as the real estate values of New York property soared, but especially after the Elevated Railroad on Third Avenue was eliminated. Jimmy's property was then suddenly worth over six million dollars. He sold the property to hungry real estate interests and retired peacefully to Palm Beach, Florida. He was, after all, a man with imagination and luck. He went from a "rubber" in a turkish bath to a retired millionaire in sunny Florida, and he engaged in an exciting business in the bargain.

As stated before, no industry was perhaps more affected at this time by the emergence of big government than the moving and storage industry. The entire relationship between the "Tiffanys," as David Brodsky calls them, and the ice man who occasionally moved someone from a cold-water flat, was decidedly changed in those years. First of all, it has been pointed out that the well-established, affluent *storage* portion of the industry did not deal with the small, local move. In the redistribution of wealth that took place in the 1930's, this business activity turned in a new direction. The moving man, whom Brodsky picturesquely describes as similar to the "lawyer chasing ambulances," never before had been competitive in the same business areas as his more influential counterpart.

Now, as the economy of the country radically changed, the two extremes started to meet literally on the street. The small operator, to whom the larger, more socially secure one might have given little thought, began now to be a force in moving and storage around the country, especially in New York City.

This enterprising mover was moving people to Park Avenue and to other fashionable areas. This change has affected today's operations: the Bowling Green and Morgan-Manhattan firms now regularly encounter trucks carrying names that they had never heard of years before. Plenty of exposure has reduced this lack of knowledge in the last 35 years.

As far as government influence was concerned, new regulations affected the relationship between the van line trying to establish its reputation with the public and the agent who was the source of business and who had traditionally maintained the personal, direct contact with the customer. Some people thought that the agent was being ousted from this relationship with the customer, but at the same time the agent needed the van line and that important nationwide coordinating service that the individual agent could not provide in the troubled 1930's.

This is where federal regulation appeared and has continued to assert itself over the years, right up to the present time, and where the investigations by the Interstate Commerce Commission in *Ex Parte* MC-19, by which the industry's practices were and are examined, have played such an important part. These investigations, the testimony, the differences of opinion — all may seem endless. However, no account of a history of the industry would be complete without their inclusion.

Some experienced observers believe that the van lines are in a far stronger position, financially, from a regulation standpoint, where they can dominate the industry beyond what is fair and equitable in relation to the agent. This is a very important question and has been so, especially since 1935.

This is another facet of the famous *Ex Parte* MC-19, which has not really been resolved since 1935. Certain basic points are still crucial to the effective resolution of this relationship between the van line and the agent.

The rate basis and, tied to it, *the commody description* were one of the first points in question. As with all important issues of these times, men had to be appointed to solve them, men who had special qualities, capabilities . . . and pressures upon them.

Griswold B. Holman was one of the key men placed in an extremely sensitive position, as far as the development of this industry is concerned. The tariff of 1935, the first industry tariff on a national basis, was set up and designed for the industry at top levels, was handled out of Washington, and was directed to a large extent by the major powers of the industry—Allied, Mayflower, North American, United, and others. To compile a workable tariff, the industry selected Holman to be the publishing agent and the overall expert in the field.

He had considerable credentials to substantiate such an important appointment. A successful warehouseman in Rutherford, New Jersey, "Gris" Holman had been brought up in the family-owned Holman Moving and Storage Company. Before entering the business, he had taken courses in transportation at the University of Pennsylvania. Over the years he had been a serious student of this industry, very much concerned with larger issues. He had reason to consider himself an expert in the moving and storage business—and many people agreed with him—because of his combination of sound academic training and many years of active experience. He was able to take an overview of the entire transportation picture.

Such confidence was also placed in him because he was one of the major Allied agents along the East Coast at a time when that geographic position carried considerable influence in the business. He was soon running the Household Goods Carriers Bureau in Washington. After his appointment, the first tariff published for the industry, the basic statement of rates and charges for the industry, was known as "The Holman Tariff."

It was a tariff that reflected the existing rate structure, in that it was figured on a cubic-foot basis. The rates were expressed in terms of dollars per cubic foot for the amount of miles traveled on each moving trip. The tariff, however, soon developed what many thought to be a serious weakness: the cubic-foot basis was completely inadequate and indefinite in establishing an accurate rate for shippers. As a result of this situation, the task of determining whether or not a customer was charged the proper rate after a delivery was practically impossible. The exact amount of the cubic footage which had been used to figure the area in the van occupied by the customer's goods was unable to be determined after the delivery was completed. If there was a complaint that the shipment was sent at an over-charged or even an undercharged rate, there was no way to check the accuracy of the rate—or on the claim that often resulted.

Because of this glaring weakness in the tariff structure, the industry cooperated in a proceeding that was initiated by the ICC, with a recommendation that all rates be expressed on a weight basis. This was the first investigation in the MC-19 series. The ICC prescribed the weight basis, at that time, for the reasons mentioned above.

After this change, the van had to be weighed both before and after it was loaded—and the net weight was used as the only basis for determining a rate. These developments took some time to pass through the federal bureaucracy. It was not until early 1939 that the first regulation tailored to the practices of the industry and its relationship with the public it served became a working law.

This was an important initial attempt to deal with the real problems of estimates—their differences in appearance and reality and the gulf between promised performance and what often actually happened on a specific move. It would be naive to think that the prescription of a regulation would eliminate this particularly sticky question. It has not. The weight basis for the rate structure still produced problems of underestimating, and it continues to be troublesome for a variety of reasons. For example, in 1969, in *Ex Parte* MC-19, the ICC revised for at least the third time the regulations relating to estimating.

Although the word "consumerism" has crept into the American language so much that it is a cliché now, the term, under other definitions, has always existed in the moving and storage business. And no matter what it is called, it represents confidence—or lack of it—between the client and the moving and storage company. This was the basis of the controversy involved in the tariff and estimate setting of the mid-1930's.

The subject of estimating and later performance on a particular estimate goes to the very source of this business. First of all, most people simply don't move as regularly and as constantly as they partake of any other service. It has been said many times that the mover has been likened to the funeral director who is called in only in times of trouble. Actually, this comparison is, of course, unduly harsh, but the point is pertinent. First, the individual shipper *must* rely on the mover to come through on his promises. Secondly, there is always an outlay of money, something that is apt to make anyone but the very rich anxious about what service he is going to get for his money. Finally, there is the question of the physical problems of moving anything. Will the goods arrive safely and on time?

This need for rapport is as important here, perhaps, as in any business. The term "estimate" then becomes a euphemism; it is simply an approach that a salesperson takes in making a sale, hoping that things will work out in the way that the salesman "hopes" they will. Of course, there are bound to be problems in this most imprecise of arts.

David Brodsky advanced the proposition recently in a speech to British moving and storage people that the two functions of sales and estimating are mutually contradictory and mutually conflicting as well; a salesman is not qualified to make an estimate by simple reason that his function is to *sell* and not to *inform*.

A man who lives by a certain percentage of what business he can bring into the moving house has to be a sterling individual not to be tempted from time to time to "hope" for certain things to happen in order to increase his amount of sales production, of which he gains a certain percentage. Not by necessarily misperforming or by deliberately misrepresenting the facts, but by slightly failing to inform completely, the salesman is placed in a key position with both the public and his own management.

The performance of this person representing the individual agent and the van line to the general consumer, therefore, is vital to the industry's public image. In the 1930's, with the publishing of tariffs that reduced this misrepresentation, the industry made an enormous breakthrough to professionalism.

Brodsky has recently commented on this very point:

"Regulation has elevated the entire tone of the industry in that it has eliminated—let's say, reduced—the incentives for underestimating by raising the general level of income and the general level of human performance. The unscrupulous operators who once worked on the fringes of the industry have been discouraged. I wouldn't say that they have been completely eliminated, of course, and a great many of them have actually gone on to conduct a higher level of business activity, a higher level of professionalism. Once you standardized your regular competition, equalized your tariffs and the rates that companies could charge people anywhere, the incentives for many of the bad practices of the past were reduced. Some of the bad practices still exist. You don't eliminate this as long as human nature is the way it is."

Events were taking place in the middle 1930's that would affect the very fabric of the moving and storage industry and the society that it served.

Highlights and ramifications of the Motor Carrier Act of 1935 were: (1) Allied Van Lines, Inc., was granted national operating authority, only if each of its cooperating firms holding such household goods authority would surrender it in favor of Allied Van Lines, Inc. (2) Three firms were granted national operating authority by the ICC under either "public convenience and necessity" or the "Grandfather" provision of the act; these firms were Aero-Mayflower Transit Company, Inc., North American Van Lines, Inc., and United Van Lines, Inc. (3) More than 4,000 firms were granted authority to haul household goods in interstate commerce on a less than national basis. (4) The ICC also ruled that it was permissible to hold such authority while participating as an agent of a firm possessing national household-goods authority.

The enactment of the Motor Carrier Act, Part II, on August 9, 1935, truly brought in a whole new era in the development of the moving and storage industry. Not only did it deal with matters involving the publication and filing of tariffs or rates, charges and practices by common carriers, but it established a forum for complaints of shippers or others. Insurance for the protection of the public was instituted, as well as the standardization of safety operations. Mergers and acquisitions of motor carriers were also regulated.

The ICC further classified movers by type of service engaged in—irregular routes with radial service, irregular routes with nonradial service and local cartage service.

In short, the business was regulated, the tariffs were standardized, and the customer, as well as the agent and van-lines operators, knew where he stood—or where they should stand with each other. Finally, the ICC classified carriers by the types of commodities which they transported. The many classifications covered are not necessary to list here, but the one most important to the moving and storage industry was "common carriers of household goods traveling over irregular routes in either radial or non-radial service." What's more, Section #206 of the Motor Carrier Act dealt with the need for a certificate of public convenience and necessity in order to operate a motor vehicle in interstate commerce. This section clearly gave the ICC control of the future expansion of public motor-carrier transportation. Of course, carriers who had been in interstate operation prior to the enactment of the Motor Carrier Act were allowed to continue in operation under the "Grandfather Clause." This has been previously described as those independent warehousemen and movers who had been engaged in the interstate moving of household goods prior to June 1, 1935. These operators, upon submitting proper application for certificates of convenience and necessity, received their "operating authority" from the ICC without any proof other than that they had been in business within the territories in which application was made on the grandfather date.

These major changes in the industry have been described with varying degrees of enthusiasm, depending on one's point of view. The operative factor was how much the laws either helped or hurt or completely failed to affect one's business. Some observers have said that the regulation was a significant and revolutionary development in the industry; while others see the provisions as only logical extensions of what would have happened normally as the business progressed through this truly significant decade in our nation's history. Whatever the eventual historical evaluation, the first reports of the ICC stressed the gigantic task involved in processing the many applications for motor-carrier operating authority sought under the "Grandfather Clause."

The scurrying around, the machinations, and the battles for power as a result of the creation of this situation are simply too numerous to mention here. However, one key consideration does merit careful attention because its effects have been felt throughout the industry's history and both favorable and unfavorable opinions are expressed, depending on where one goes in the industry.

It was with Allied Van Lines that the ICC took a position that differed somewhat from that relating to Aero-Mayflower, United Van Lines, North American Van Lines, and other leaders. It is necessary, for a clear explanation of this complicated case, to go ahead to the outcome of the situation before giving its specific causes. On February 5, 1946, Allied was denied a certificate of convenience and necessity under both Sections #206 Grandfather Clause and #207 of the ICC Act because the Commission viewed Allied, organized as it was as a nonprofit cooperative, as an agent for its several independent carrier members rather than viewing these several carriers as agents of Allied. Allied was ordered to cease and desist its interstate activities, effective July 1, 1946.

The tremors of the Allied decision are still felt today. There were strong feelings everywhere in the business, no matter what one's direct relationship to Allied was. Government ruling in this decision went deep to the heart of the management of the country's largest van line. Tempers flare even today at mention of the subject. That the issue was first raised in the 1930's was only a prelude to later decisions that occurred in the next decade.

Here is how the ICC reasoned: a key consideration was the fact that prior to July 1, 1935, and even after that date, Allied Van Lines had operated fully as a nonprofit cooperative venture associated with the National Furniture Warehousemen's Association. The ICC ruled that Allied had not functioned as a carrier but rather *acted* as an agent, and it had served merely as a clearing house for return loads on behalf of its independent members. The ICC further pointed out that many of the Allied members had been granted, or were in the process of applying for, their own interstate operating authority.

This denial of interstate operating authority naturally faced Allied with a very serious problem both for Allied and for its members. This particular denial came after an earlier ruling of the ICC which had denied Allied and its members application to pool certain traffic, service, gross and net earnings, operating rights, and properties. The membership of Allied Van Lines voted that application should be made with the ICC to allow Allied Van Lines to purchase the operating rights owned by existing members of Allied. In April, 1946, the ICC approved and authorized Allied Van Lines' request to purchase the household-goods operating rights of 325 named motor-vehicle common carriers.

It was further implied that if an independent mover were to stay a member—or an agent—of Allied Van Lines, he must surrender to the van line his operating authority. This caused owners of many firms to do some serious soul searching and project their thinking into long-range planning. As a result, several agent firms left Allied Van Lines, Inc., and many old and valued business relationships were severed. A group of these firms formed, with a similar group from United Van Lines, an organization known as the Committee for Preservation of Carrier Rights. They began to negotiate for the purchase of all the outstanding stock of United Van Lines, Inc. This purchase was completed on March 17, 1947. Later, the ICC entered proceedings against both North American Van Lines, Inc., and United Van Lines, Inc., following the decision affecting the Allied situation on pooling, etc. After much long investigation, control of these national carriers by some of their carrier agent firms and pooling agreements with these and noncontrolling carrier agent firms were approved.

Throughout the 1930's all businesses were affected by strong central government. Perhaps for the first time in the nation's history decisions now came from "Big Brother" in Washington, and not from the man who had to meet his payroll each week.

Also, in the mid-thirties, there was a battle about approving a proposed order removing the moving trucks of the country from the Household Goods Storage and Moving Trade Code and placing them under the Trucking Code. This possibility, as Martin Kennelly, President, Werner-Kennelly, Chicago, Illinois, pointed out in a strong letter to W. Averell Harriman, then administrative officer of the National Recovery Administration, would terminate the Household Goods Storage and Moving Trade Code. As Kennelly argued, his business and that of his associates had been organized into associations as long ago as 1897. The business of moving and storage was a *trade* — and the industry was entitled *to its own code*. The point was well taken and the industry won the battle of the code, a conspicuous victory.

There would soon be enormous government controls made necessary by a world fast coming apart at the seams. At the beginning of 1939, Barcelona fell to Franco, and the Spanish Civil War ended in a Falange victory. In March, Germany overran Czechoslovakia and in April, Mussolini decided to shore up his failing fortunes at home by crushing tiny Albania.

On April 30, the New York World's Fair opened.

There were light moments: The King and Queen of England made a visit to this country in June, and the Roosevelts, at a party given at the White House, served hot dogs.

In August, Germany and Russia signed a nonaggression pact very soon to be broken. On September 1, 1939, to signal the end of a decade and the start of an even bloodier one, Hitler's armies invaded Poland. On the third of September, England declared war on the Third Reich.

At the close of the 1930's and with the increased role of government in the operations of the moving and storage industry, it was thought by most observers that the general situation would at least be stabilized for a while. Regardless of how one thought about the rightness or the wrongness of the government's presence, the future could be reasonably predicted. Suddenly, with the rise of fascism in Europe and the Far East, the world was destined to go through its worst ordeal to date. The government was forced to control the moving and storage industry even more than usual because of the effort to win World War II.

The world was going through violent change. However, the moving and storage industry was only starting to see the era of its biggest challenges and growth—the era of World War II, the mobile society in all its complexities and the fantastic growth of postwar expansion, in terms of the personal family move, the corporate move, and the military move. And this change was, as always, a reflection of the times in general. The world was in ferment, and the moving and storage business had come of age. It had to grow in order to perform the gigantic tasks asked of it.

4

The War

The year 1940 saw some quite amazing reversals in power: In barely twelve months' time, Hitler threw his armies against Belgium and the Netherlands, outflanked the reputedly invincible Maginot Line—and within six weeks reduced and bludgeoned all three nations into submission. The British army which in September of 1939 went into battle with stiff upper lip and high morale was reduced to near annihilation in June on the beach at Dunkirk.

In America we saw things change, but much more comfortably. Industry was slowly recovering from the Depression and the government was exerting more control over every phase of industry.

To anyone with any inside knowledge about the real story of Washington and its activities, it was no secret that many changes were taking place in the government that would soon affect the whole country. President Roosevelt had called certain business and transportation leaders to Washington in the early fall of that year to talk about the approaching crisis in Europe and the various aggressive movements of the Japanese in the

Pacific. In September, 1940, FDR declared an official state of limited emergency. Top leaders in the rubber, oil, and transportation industries were making regular trips to call on Secretary of the Interior Harold Ickes and other cabinet ministers. The times were dire but exciting too in the nation's capital.

It was at this time that President Roosevelt was in the process of winning an unprecedented third term. He was campaigning vigorously (some felt hypocritically) to "keep our boys out of war." As a result, the attention of the nation that autumn was fixed on this national election as never before. Both the Republican and Democratic parties were internally divided between the isolationists, who wanted nothing whatsoever to do with the troubles in Europe and the Far East, and the interventionists, who wanted the United States to become immediately involved in the War overseas.

The Republican Convention, for example, was stampeded by a spontaneous sentiment that swept a forceful speaker with a shock of unruly hair to international prominence. His name was Wendell Willkie and he spoke for the philosophy of "One World." He wanted to make sure that FDR "Never Won a Third Term." Throughout the campaign one also heard the rantings of Adolf Hitler, whose shouting voice made it abundantly clear that he was bent on world conquest.

Closer to home than this long-distance warning was the effect that the massive Transportation Act had on the moving and storage industry. One section made it "no longer mandatory for government agencies to advertise for bids in connection with the procurement of transportation services when such services can be procured from any common carrier lawfully operating in a territory where the services are to be performed."

It was further noted that "the law does not make mandatory, but merely *permits,* the elimination of bids and the selection of qualified carriers on the basis of published tariffs."

The immediate effects on the industry were largely in doubt, but one thing was certain: the government was now going to operate under slightly less chaotic conditions than prevailed before, with respect to carrier operations in handling government removals.

The new law gave voice to many industry spokesmen who were virtually unanimous in extolling the good effects the law should have. J. F. Rowan, Executive Secretary of the Household Goods Carriers Bureau, commented at the time: "It will behoove all motor common carriers to gain the widest press publicity to this new development, in order to quickly eliminate the evils which have beset the industry because of the past bid procedure, demanded only from motor carriers."

The response was real and so were the results, in a country fast preparing for the biggest war in its history. The effects on the moving business were immediate, especially in those parts of the country that contained important military installations. In November of 1940, the movement of the personnel of Hamilton Field to Fort Douglas in Utah due to "the decision of the War Department to reorganize and decentralize all air fields in the United States" created a moving job of the largest proportions. Bekins Van and Storage of San Francisco was awarded the job. Several firms participated in the contract. Among them were Pierce Rodolph Storage Company and Yelloway Van Lines of San Francisco, California; Ace Van and Storage of San Diego, California; Cole Transfer of Ogden, Utah; Redman Van Lines and Mollerup Van Lines of Salt Lake City, Utah; and the United Van Lines of Cleveland, Ohio.

The transfer of the 7th Bombardment Group, made up of 105 officers, 841 men with 25 four-motored bombers of the "Flying Fortress" type, along with 39 men of the 88th Reconnaissance and 15 men of the 5th Air Base, presented the largest physical moving job of household goods and personal effects that had ever been handled in the West, according to the November, 1940, issue of *The Furniture Warehouseman.*

These early assignments were merely a prelude to the gigantic logistical movements that lay ahead in North Africa and Europe.

As many historians have pointed out, American logistical

support was critical in the waging of the War. The United States simply knew how to get to the right spot with the right amount of people and goods—before the enemy did. A large share of this success was brought about by moving and storage men who were called into service and who did the job that had to be done. It is also true that the expertise learned in military life can be applied directly to civilian life. Many men easily made the transition from military moving work to an assignment of the same kind in their postwar occupations at home. The experience was often valuable.

All was not completely grim at the time that our country was preparing for War. In New York, the venerable jeweler, Tiffany, planned to move from its 37th Street location to new quarters at 57th Street and Fifth Avenue—where it still stands today. Selected to do the job was Byrnes Brothers of New York City. The move involved the transfer of articles worth over $10,000,000. The list of objects included: 1,500 silver ashtrays, 3,500 rings, one of the largest stocks of imported china in New York—and the finest stock of diamonds, pearls, and precious stones in the world. *The New Yorker* magazine saw fit to honor the move with a major story that described the Tiffany operations as the most complicated move in New York City's history. Except for 1,500 watches and 15,000 pieces of jewelry which were taken uptown in three trips by an armored car—and not including some valuable records and papers that Tiffany executives transported in their own pockets—*all* of Tiffany's stock, office furnishings, and other belongings were involved.

Two $3,500 vases were transported in special, extra-size containers (the most valuable barrel load contained $8,500 worth of china). The most valuable box load contained $100,-000 of silver, including an antique teapot that was priced at $4,500.

There were 30 packers and supply packers on the job constantly. What was the difference between the two? "Packers pack," said Jimmy O'Neill, President of Byrnes Brothers, "and supply packers supply the packers with things to pack."

For Byrnes Brothers, the move was routine. The firm had

once hoisted a 30-foot directors' table up 52 floors in mid-Manhattan and through a window in the Radio Corporation of America's building. Byrnes Brothers had moved bones around in Trinity Churchyard in downtown New York. The company had also moved the stock of the famous art dealer, Lord Duveen, shortly before, from New York to London. "That was a $350,000 job—and damage claims came to $5.95. In the Tiffany move, the ratio of damage was even better—only three inexpensive cups and two inexpensive glasses were broken in the whole operation," said O'Neill.

It would be nice if all the moves made necessary at the time were as pleasant as the Tiffany move, but wartime conditions were beginning to prevail. In October of 1940, The Soldiers' and Sailors' Relief Act provided "temporary suspension of legal proceedings and transactions which may prejudice the civil rights of persons in such service during the period herein specified over which the Act remains in force."

In an exposition published by Roy James Mills, a prominent Chicago attorney, the pattern was obvious as to the important effects the Act would have on the entire moving and storage industry.

The "general tenor," stated Mr. Mills, "would indicate that it was the purpose of the Congress to provide for relief in such instances as affected by the Act." Section #200 provides that no default judgment may be entered without the plaintiff and the mover first filing an affidavit indicating (a) that the defendant is in military service; (b) that the defendant is *not* in military service; or (c) that the plaintiff does not know whether or not the defendant is in military service.

"It will then be seen that the provisions of the Act place the burden upon those seeking to enforce a civil right to prove that the party whom they are proceeding against is not in military service," said Mills.

"If the one seeking to enforce a civil remedy is unable truthfully to make an affidavit as to whether or not the defendant is in military service, he must post a bond to indemnify the defendant in military service against any loss or damage that he may suffer by reason of any judgment, should the judgment thereafter be set aside. . . ."

The moving and storage business was clearly in the War and would continue to be throughout, in terms of storage and sales of servicemen's goods that directly affected a clientele that was largely disrupted, or at least radically changed. The absence of customers and the customers' goods for great periods of time, due to overseas assignments and other hardships, would continue to produce situations that no one could foresee or prevent.

Much was to happen so quickly that the industry, as well as the people who operated it, didn't know what to expect next. In January, 1941, Franklin Roosevelt announced the Four Freedoms and, with the advent of Lend Lease, was pouring more than seven billion dollars a year into the United States economy. Other countries, like Great Britain and Russia, were being helped enormously by the United States.

Discussion of the War was everywhere. Japan signed a non-aggression pact with the Soviet Union. Such adverse feeling existed against Japan that the President called for a voluntary embargo against that country, one that left Japan with only two years of oil on hand, for example, and seven months of aluminum. It was a situation that was bound to end in violence.

In August, FDR and Winston Churchill met at sea, and later as a result of that historic meeting, issued the famous Atlantic Charter, a combination of FDR's own New Deal philosophy and clearly reflecting the pressure that both he and Churchill were undergoing because of the rushing tide of fascist pressure in every part of the world. The Charter had enormous popular appeal and received huge play in the world press. It was unofficially a pact to help Britain in the War. America was therefore committed, whether the average person realized it or not. During that same month of August, the Office of Supply, Priorities and Allocations was created, and the Roosevelt Administration was well along in a plan to raise an army of at least 8,000,000 men.

The effects on the economy and the moving and storage industry were inescapable. By October, the Germans were within 100 miles of Moscow and United States material aid was flowing freely to the Russians, as well as to the British. Late in October, the President asked for something that seemed incredible at the time: 50,000 airplanes—and 50,000 airplanes to be produced almost immediately. At the very time FDR was speaking to the nation, one of our submarines, the *Kearny,* was torpedoed in the Atlantic Ocean. Whether we liked it or not, knew it or not, or faced up to the enormous changes the War would make on every one of our American lives, we were heading for a death struggle with the Axis powers. And these powers soon gave us every excuse to wage war against them. That reason was Pearl Harbor. We now were in a battle for survival, with no holds barred.

Aside from the obvious dislocation, migration, and various eruptions that the beginning of World War II caused, the changes in the moving business were just as dramatic. But in some ways, in the throes of change, the industry was solidifying, too, for it would never be quite the same again.

Although there is no apparent direct relationship between the United States involvement in World War II and the formation of the thousands of interstate household goods carriers, it was during this period that many of their financial and operating structures and philosophies were moulded.

No generalizations can be made about every one of the thousands of firms in the business, but a study of *four* national carriers bears significance in order to understand how things operated at that time.

A study of these four companies will show how they were set up and how they functioned: On one end of the spectrum is the closely held Aero-Mayflower Transit Company, Inc., with ownership that is clearly separated from the agent firms which represent the corporation; and on the other end is the firm that has had so much to do with shaping the trends of the industry and must necessarily appear in any history like this—Allied

Van Lines, Inc. All Allied's stock is held by its agent firms, which, as a whole, make up about one-half of all that carrier's agencies.

At the other end of the spectrum we see North American Van Lines, Inc., joining Aero-Mayflower on the chart, in that a large percentage of its ownership is distinct from the national carrier's agent firms. North American has seen even more "non-domination" by its agent firms, sometimes even arranging special contracts for treatment for some stockholder agents. Then, with the merger of North American with Pepsi Co., Inc., the carrier's ownership became even further removed from any hint of domination by agent firms of the North American Van Lines, Inc. company.

On the other hand, as far as our chart is concerned, United Van Lines, Inc., is extremely close to the operating philosophy of Allied, because in their mutual past histories they present similar patterns. United was purchased and reorganized by relatively small household goods carriers which had, with only a few exceptions, been associated with Allied Van Lines, Inc. Although United is not a "no-profit corporation," it is entirely owned by a significant group of its agent firms which hold equal portions of that ownership interest.

It is important to point out that the basis for this rather arbitrary "visual" pairing has been a consideration of that portion of the national carrier's ownership which rests with a broad base of the national carrier's agents; for it is this factor which has had the greatest effect on the operating philosophy of these major carriers—not *how widely the common stock of these firms is dispersed.*

As might be expected, the operating philosophies of such varying firms can also be divided into two groups. Aero-Mayflower and North American believe that interstate household goods transportation is the business or service of the national carrier. Providing such service is the national carrier's responsibility, and *not* the responsibility of the local agent firm. It is the objective of these two national carriers to provide interstate household goods moving services at a reasonable profit, which will afford a reasonable rate of return on their equity interests. . . .

A basic difference within this first operating philosophy is that Aero-Mayflower uses a system of granting exclusive agency contracts to one firm in a given geographic area, while North American has tried to build up an agency by the granting of contracts to several agencies in larger metropolitan markets.

The second type of national carrier philosophy, as it was indicated several years ago in an industry study, is the one basically reflected by both United and Allied. In this case, the national carrier was created for the benefit of the agent firms which form their ownership. These stockholder agent firms see their local firms as interstate household goods carriers. Originally they needed a national firm, through which they could cooperate in providing better service for their customers while furnishing return loads for one another. The agent firms in such an organization as Allied, for example, clearly realize that their rights and privileges as stockholder agents are obtained *only* by giving up the right to do hauling on their own interstate authority.

As many business reporters have pointed out, in neither Allied Van Lines, Inc., nor in United Van Lines, Inc., is the profitability of the national carrier of the greatest value and importance, because the profit producer and the center of this profit, which the stockholders hold as the most important factor, is the *income statement* of the local firm which serves as the carrier's agent. So, the stockholders would appear to view their stock interest in the national carrier as an important operating asset . . . and not as an investment in a security. This basic relationship goes to the heart of all operating procedures — the providing of equipment, the handling of accounts receivable, the providing of warehouse facilities — and the nature of agent-firm compensation. Of course this description applies to only four leaders, while many hundreds of companies around the country operate differently.

One should also mention here the completely independent

operator and those few carriers who believe they can own all their own agencies, while many others fall into variations of the operating structures and philosophies of the four carriers described above.

Great social and economic changes were taking place all over the country, especially in the middle and lower economic classes. Never had so many people moved from their homes to take new jobs. "Rosie the Riveter" was not just an idle song. Women did the work of men, were paid like men.

Such upward mobility into economic opportunity did not come in simple or pleasurable terms to everyone. It was during these years that the great migrations of workers took place in the South, for example, to the Northeastern mills and factories and especially to Chicago, which seems to attract every kind of element in America—all perhaps because it is in the middle of the flow. . . . North and South, East and West.

The eminent University of Chicago demographer, Dr. Philip Hauser, in an interview, recently pointed out that in Holmes County, Mississippi, once called "the poorest county in America," more change has been noticeable than in almost any part of the world. For example, sharecropping became even more precarious than before; the War plants of the North and of Chicago beckoned. First, the father went up North and then the older brothers, and then the whole family would follow. More families moved during that time, and since, from that rural poverty-stricken corner of Mississippi to the West End and the Maywood sections of Chicago than to any other place in the country. Mammoth studies have been written about the migration, and it is easy to see why. There was enormous hope that things would be better.

Since the affluent middle and upper-middle class also moved to take governmental and War-related jobs, the country was in constant movement. Dr. Hauser has also commented that since World War II at least one billion people have migrated, either from country to country, or from state to state, inside the boundaries of the United States.

Changes brought about by these extensive movements of

people and all the goods they carry with them are not only physical. There are subtle and ubiquitous biosocial adaptations — ones that sometimes work and sometimes don't. Involved in this migration have been the factors of increased congestion, noise pollution, traffic snarls, and climatic wrenches that put an Eskimo, for example, in wretched isolation in a climate like that of Southern California. There is the impersonality of urban living that often seems downright sadistic, if not merely strange, to a previous dweller in the country.

More restrictions of every kind were made necessary by urban congestion. This situation affected the moving and storage man in the way he operated his business, in large and small ways. Crowded conditions made it difficult to move household goods down packed city streets. More apartment building residences than before, the advent of 20- and 30-story highrise apartments, and more traffic and parking restrictions presented new challenges to movers who were, perhaps, used to working with people who moved most of the time to and from single, private residences, either in the same town or in a different city.

Everywhere one was to see the role of the government in all lives. In fact, the warehouseman was cautioned in an article in *The Furniture Warehouseman* that he might not make a sale of a serviceman's goods with safety. "Until there are decisions definitely made, the only safe procedure is to wait until the termination of military service and three months thereafter before conducting a sale of goods belonging to a known individual in military service."

The article goes on to point out that conditions had permanently changed in the American psyche. We can assume even more than the author of this article that the industry saw the handwriting on the wall: "Of course, each warehouseman must determine for himself what chances he wishes to take. So long as the public is willing to believe, however, that a condition of emergency exists, the tenor of public opinion and the opinion of judges will be such that any case involving the slightest sus-

picion that a draftee is being treated unfairly will be handled
very summarily. The warehouseman who permits himself to be
placed in a position where it will appear that he is persecuting
a draftee will receive very slight consideration."

The industry learned, grew, and prospered—at home and
overseas. The truck was used everywhere. It later was the
vehicle that somehow made it through the hot churning sands of
North Africa, the mud of Italy, and the flames of bombed-out
Germany . . . to its destination, where the goods had to be used.

During the 1920's and 1930's, miracles were being performed in the laboratories of chemical companies—within the
United States and abroad. Germany, after the First World War,
sought to avoid the shortages of natural rubber and petroleum
products that had so hindered it in its unsuccessful attempt
to wage World War I. It would try to rectify those weaknesses.
During the 1930's, the industrial world had been rocked by the
magnificent rumors and often real factual reports about fabled
German efficiency and capacity to develop synthetic rubber
and petroleum products . . . a condition that might render the
country invincible in another war.

The Russians, monumental in their suspiciousness, were often led into believing the news of German industrial exploits.
If fuel was so plentiful and easy to come by after these Brave
New World experiments, then the aggressive Germans would
not *need* to come into the oil-rich Caucasus for materials and
resources, or so the Russians hoped.

Of course, this was not the case. Germany's size alone, in
comparison to Russia and the United States, for instance, is
miniscule. The entire German oil industry consumed, at the
time of these experiments, only 5% of the normal peacetime requirements of the United States of America alone.

Where then was a warlike nation, aggressive in its needs for
vital resources and predestined to military conquest, to turn for
more materials? To the outside of course, and to the oil-rich
and rubber-rich areas of the world that both Germany and
Japan must dominate. It was in these areas that the Allies had

to protect their needs for their vital resources. The moving and storage industry, specifically tied to the needs of these vital resources of oil and rubber, was to face the wartime shortages, while at the same time meeting increased government and private demands for greater service.

In April, 1942, the Japanese captured the Burmese capitol of Rangoon and, in a later air strike on Ceylon, sank the British aircraft carrier *Hermes,* two big cruisers, and many smaller vessels. In Southeast Asia (where our role was inextricably involved with the need for resources), the Japanese sank the British heavy cruiser *Repulse* and that grand new battleship of the sea, *The Prince of Wales.* In fact, the efficiency of this tiny nation, Japan, was never higher. In a few months time, the Japanese effectively destroyed the supremacy of the British Royal Navy for all time.

Back home, the waterways, as well as the roads of the country, were as busy as gas rationing would allow. People were involved in the great interior migration, that grand movement of troops and material to every coastal town, to every part of the country. From corn field to Cape Cod, from Utah to California, the country was on the move.

In the Mississippi Valley area, more action was to be seen than Mark Twain might ever have imagined. Towboats, barges —all were being met at the various docks up and down the great river by trucks carrying every kind of commodity that could be thought of. *And* all the people involved in the moves to debarkation points possessed household goods. In the eyes of many observers, the industry never worked harder. The wage and price freeze again demonstrated the controls of the government on the moving and storage industry. This condition produced an ambivalent and frustrating experience. On one hand, the business had never had more need for its services—its people were never busier—but the controls on prices kept profits down and wage stability made it more than usually necessary to keep more men on the payroll at even higher wages than previously paid. The result was a busy, often frantic, activity producing less than optimum profits. The role of management was a tough one then, and many lessons were learned that were later applied when the War was over.

The industry's attention to keeping service at the highest level was constantly called for. The abundance of moving jobs, the absence of trained people, the tendency for people to neglect their selling skills when they didn't have to use them—all conditions called for the greatest diligence.

Full employment, and the creation of new skills and new standards of living for millions of people, brought in an age of affluence that we today take for granted.

Any account of those violent times must carry thousands of difficult, well-handled, and dramatic moves of people and goods from one place to another. The big picture is always made up of individual dots of color in the canvas. In Washington, for example, the arduous organization of the military operation called upon the best skills of experienced moving professionals. Early in the defense of the country, the Security Storage and Van Corporation, Norfolk, Virginia, was given the important job of moving the Air Corps (as it was known then) "GHQ," the nerve center of air operations, from Langley Field, near Norfolk, to Bolling Field, on the outskirts of Washington, D.C. The challenge was that government officials insisted that the move be completed in 63 hours, while making sure that at no time would the nerve center of communications be out of commission. The job was handled successfully in 29 hours. Working in connection with Allied Van Lines, Security got 16 Allied vans which were ready for work at 7 A.M. on the given day of the move. By noon of the next day these 16 vans had completed the removal of 57 tons of equipment—including radio and communications machinery, files of maps, records, and other documents—and all office furniture and other physical properties, including a 7,000-pound photostat machine. All the material was moved, in this short period of time, more than 190 miles.

The need for the centralization of this delicate communications equipment in the Washington, D.C., area called on Security Storage and Van's highest skills, ones that were later used by many other branches of the armed forces.

This isolated but important incident points up the widening use of the moving and storage industry at that time by defense contractors and the later growth in this special class of moving in following years. The industries involved in the War effort were shipping every sort of device, large and small, to help troops in all parts of the world. The moving executive, by satisfying these special demands of the military, was learning valuable lessons for profitable activity in the years ahead.

In February, 1943, the annual meeting of the NFWA held at Chicago's Edgewater Beach Hotel was appropriately devoted to the theme: *War Problems Conference.* Prior to that time it had been impossible for industry members to meet and to discuss the general and specific issues that every one of them faced. The meeting was for the express purpose of discussing operating, legislative, and servicing problems of warehousing and moving "gauged to the demands of the War." The convention held in 1942 was really too close to the shock of Pearl Harbor and America's entry into the world conflict. The 1943 meeting was then the first chance to get to the heart of certain complex problems that had been facing the industry.

For example, members knew by that time of the acute shortage of personnel, and they wanted to know how their associates were meeting their challenges in other parts of the country.

They were also aware, very painfully in several cases, that government agencies by legislative directive were requiring of them a vast amount of record-keeping and compliance to federal and state regulations. Were there any possible shortcuts or exemptions? What were the other members facing that could be used as common experience and as a source for common wisdom?

Equipment was fast wearing out. What could be done, in view of the fact that new equipment was virtually impossible to find? Still, people and materials had to move. What steps could be taken to conserve and maintain costly units that had to last for the War's duration?

Perhaps most importantly members were greatly aware of the changes made necessary in previously existing methods of cost control and accounting. New taxes, new costs, and high *gross* incomes (but not necessarily net) were making a shambles of any orderly analysis of the reality behind operating procedures. Were there ways to know what was *real* profit, what *real* costs were in respect to income? All these considerations, and specifically the accounting and cost-analysis items, were high on everyone's priority list. (It is interesting to see that in such a volatile, changing industry the questions of *real* accounting and the availability of quality personnel have topped almost every list of priority topics that industry leaders discuss today, either formally, as part of a written agenda, or informally in conversation at social gatherings from Boca Raton, Florida, to the Century Plaza Hotel in Los Angeles, California.)

The lines for discussion were drawn: "The battle strategy for the household goods storage and moving industry during the crucial months of 1943 will be developed at the NFWA War Problems Conference," stated the industry publication of that month. "Specific information on the perplexing wartime phases of operating warehouses will be available, to provide every warehouseman who attends with armament that should stand him in good stead when he attacks his individual operating problems."

To Chicago then went the industry, and the imagery of the broadside announcing this historic meeting could not have been more fitting. "Battle strategy, crucial months, armament attacks . . ."—these terms appeared in a variety of ways on the meeting's agenda.

Making more of the talents of women in the moving and storage industry figured much in the discussions, a consideration that might have earlier been made, in order to deal effectively with the largely feminine problems of moving a household. In other words, women could be very effective in handling claims for other women clients. Also, the delicate jobs of packing fine china and other *bric-a-brac* cried out for the light female touch.

In this regard, Bekins was doing a great deal in the West, according to a story published in *The Furniture Warehouseman* of September, 1943, while on the East Coast, J. H. Evans and Sons of White Plains, New York, had been doing an outstanding job.

Women were also filling management positions at the time, in order to assume important vacancies when moving executives were drafted or when they enlisted in the armed forces. Perhaps this development was indeed the forerunner of "Mothers' Truckers" and other such modern concerns operating around the country—inside and outside of Greenwich Village in New York. The way one feels about Women's Lib seems to be academic. Women took on a job at that crucial time and performed well. They are continuing to do so, both inside and outside the warehouse or moving firm.

The industrial trade press was reacting somewhat the same way to women during wartime, in all parts of America. The ladies were necessary to do the job—and they were doing it. In May, 1943, the *Greater New York Movers News* commented: "Along the entire war front woman is playing an important part and will continue to be more and more important as we get deeper into the War. We doff our hats to these women. . . . Right in our own industry we have a complement of women whom we will match against any others for competence. Since World War I, when by necessity, wives and sisters took over for their warrior brothers and husbands, the moving and storage business has been proud to list on its roster scores of women who are doing a big job and doing it well. We know that every male member of our industry will echo our cheer for the women in our trade."

Aside from gallant statements like these, hard reality was showing that women were making it in a tough business. According to some figures on employment increases published later that year, women constituted 9.2% of all employees in the warehousing field.

In fact, the entire business was beside itself with a need for competent help, regardless of sex. Between March 1 and September 1 of 1943, it was estimated that 37,073 additional jobs would have to be reckoned with for the entire trucking industry. To a limited extent, these openings could be filled by men past military age, but the considerable majority were to be found in women's groups, where previously no such opportunity existed. That this condition worked well for many far-sighted firms hardly needs to be discussed. Since that time, with admittedly mixed results, women have taken on more responsibility.

So many far-reaching trends were begun during the War concerning the industry's responsiveness and its contributions to the War effort, that it is difficult, if not impossible, to relate all of the most important or touching or dramatic.

One incident could be considered indicative of this industry-wide involvement in the War effort. Lyon Van and Storage Company had long been a leader in West Coast operations, and their trucks with the slogan "Let Lyon Guard Your Goods" were well known for years to motorists up and down Pacific Coast highways. In the early part of the War, Lyon started its own aeronautical division and had actually operated its own airport, one that was completely equipped to disassemble, pack, and crate planes and plane parts for transoceanic shipment. In many instances, as many as 56 separate major operations were necessary on each engine to prepare a plane for shipment to a battle zone. Because security was paramount in the operation, not all the specifics could be related, but some general description of the jobs performed might show the degree of involvement in this important work.

As Austin Hathaway, the general manager of the Lyon Aeronautical Division, related it: "Each of the 56 major operations may require a performance of up to 20 smaller operations before it is finally considered complete. Our men are expert aviation mechanics and can handle a plane's engine almost with their eyes closed. . . . We know that every part must be in top working condition when the plane arrives at the battle front. For a poorly conditioned part may spell the difference between life and death for one or more of our boys. . . . Boiled down, our job is to preserve and condition the engines and parts, the propeller and propeller shaft, the armament, automatic pilots, gyros, the wings, and fuselage. And finally, to transport the planes to the docks for shipping."

As many as 500 men of Lyon worked at various assembly points, as well as at its own airport at Alhambra, California. Even though the men and many of the executives at Lyon didn't ever know where in the world the fruits of their labors might show up, they were well aware of the dangerous jobs their work was fitting the planes for. As Mr. Hathaway's words show, the men of Lyon felt they were contributing a great deal to a life-and-death struggle.

As discussed previously, such delicate operations, which before had been outside the usual confines of the moving and storage business, made for greater opportunities after the War. Along the Pacific Coast Lyon and others were active. Meanwhile, on the East Coast, such firms as the Davidson Transfer & Storage Co. of Baltimore, the Quaker Transit Co. of Philadelphia, and the Seven Santini Brothers were performing the same unique feats packing enormous quantities of parts and equipment for shipment to servicemen in Europe, Africa, and on the east coast of South America.

By contributing and growing with this responsibility the industry increased its knowledge and eventually prospered after the War was over.

At midwartime, an overview of the moving and storage situation was offered by *The Wall Street Journal* — and it was not serene: "Moving day, 1943, is likely to be the most hectic in history, a recent coast-to-coast survey shows." That was the lead sentence and the rest of the article backed up this first impression with hard facts and statistics.

"There is evidence that almost as many thousands of New

Yorkers as usual intend to swap dwellings during the traditional September 15 to October 1 (lease renewals), with only half as much muscle to do the toting. In Los Angeles, where there is no traditional moving time, activity is reported already at a record level."

Other cities like Pittsburgh and Chicago were in equally bad fixes. The moving jam was coming all at one time and there were not enough helpers to go around. In Los Angeles, women were used as "moving men," even though they didn't have to carry heavy pianos up five flights of steps. They were, however, doing almost everything else. Storage was at an absolute premium. On the West Coast, War workers' families arrived to set up their households, could not find a decent place to live, and so decided to put their things into storage. This was going on all over the country, also. Drafted husbands were sending their brides back to their parents' homes to live, piling furniture aboard vans and dispatching them to storage space that in many cases didn't even exist.

In Chicago, where in 1943 storage areas were filled only to 80% capacity, there was a widespread fear about the future — if many more husbands and fathers were drafted from the Chicago area. Chicago warehouses had been deluged with inquiries about what was going to happen next. Most companies predicted that widespread future drafting of men would cause the remaining 20% space to be quickly gobbled up.

In Washington, D.C., few people made any plans to move that year at all. "There was simply no place in the inn," said one prominent real estate broker at the time. "In fact, there's no place to move, except to the curb," said a real estate man interviewed by *The Wall Street Journal*. Further, there were only 65 to 70% of the usual amount of available moving men. And the ones actively engaged were constantly busy with the huge federal government projects that so occupied the established firms in the Washington area. Fifty men of one company were counted at one time busily moving the National Labor Relations Board from one part of town to another.

In Washington at that time, C. A. Aspinwall of Security Storage Company reported: "We are getting a liberal education in geography here by making shipments for the many government officers and clerks going to all parts of the world. They all have to fly and, hence, their baggage has to be shipped. Checking their orders for today, I noticed one for La Paz, Bolivia, one for Bogotá, Colombia, another for Managua, Nicaragua—one for Jidda, Saudi Arabia—four for Algiers. . . ."

The huge demands of War had met a situation in which an industry was badly lacking in competent help. For instance, at the beginning of 1941, in New York City, the International Brotherhood of Teamsters, Chauffeurs, Warehousemen and Helpers of America had 5,679 members. In October of 1943 it had 2,714 members. At the same time that these figures were being supplied to *The Wall Street Journal,* the New York Telephone Company was reporting that 83% more phones would be moved from one address to another in 1943 than in 1941. This situation occurred at the time of a drop in manpower of around 48%, compared with the 1941 level.

More work and fewer workers made for an almost chaotic situation in most of the urban centers of the country. By today's standards, costs would not be considered astronomical, but in those days some costs and extra charges could be quite painful. In high-rise apartments, for example, clients had to wait for space in a single freight elevator, and often moving men simply had to sit in the hallways, running up a bill of $100 without doing anything at all.

To alleviate this situation, everyone was urged to move as soon as possible, and not wait for the usual lease renewal period and the accompanying glut of people and their goods journeying from one apartment to another. Early in the War a bill was introduced in the New York State legislature, designed to reform the hectic situation, but the bill did not get far. In Chicago also, moving men pushed for a staggering of the traditional moving dates long in existence there. They were unable to get any concrete action from the local real estate boards. As a result of regular semiannual moving dates in that city, some pooling of loads was accomplished by members of the local movers associations. Larger firms, which usually had orders well in advance, notified extra clients to contact the movers association which in turn diverted these extra orders to less well-known firms which did not have the overflow of work that the established firms had.

Of course, compared with the hardships of wartime in Europe and Asia, waiting for one's household goods for several weeks' time seems small indeed in terms of human suffering.

Wartime trends did set a definite pattern for some of the problems to come: overwork at the exact same time of year, the problem of return loads, and the use of available manpower in the most economic ways.

These questions have still not been reconciled, of course. The Second World War simply exasperated many executives and continually reminded them of perennial problems that *must* be resolved, somehow, sometime in the near future. However, more professional training of personnel than existed at that time has been carried out. Better planning in the return load problem area, for example, with the help of increased computerization, has reduced these problems. Many industry leaders would like to see much more of this professionalism.

"Normal operations" would never be an accurate term for this particular industry again. What is more, many industry leaders were searching their own minds and asking questions out loud about the future — after the War. What would happen; what could be done to make things work better?

Eric Dahl, director of sales promotion for Allied, delivered a paper in 1944 that was especially referred to around the industry about the trends of the times as he saw them then and as he expected they would change the old way of doing things.

After first allowing that the industry's major responsibility was to the War effort and to the conservation of tires, trucks, and other essential equipment, Dahl went on to make some other sensible points: "The tremendous industrial development of the Southwest," he said, "due to the decentralization of War industries, is just one indication of the changing economy to be expected after the War. We do not have to do any crystal gazing to be aware of certain facts and questions that must be answered. Unless we do look ahead now there is danger that we may become neither the masters nor the servants, but merely the *victims* of the future. . . . Let's ask a few pertinent questions: What are you going to do with the warehouse space that will be empty as a result of the removal of goods stored for the duration? Have you made plans to replace the equipment that has been wearing out these past two years? What improvements in design for greater utility and economy do you wish to include when purchasing new equipment? Have you thought about jobs for former employees who are presently with the armed services? What are the railroads going to do to build up tonnage they are bound to lose with the end of hostilities, and will their guns be pointed in our direction? What about air cargo and its possibilities as far as your business is concerned?"

That these questions were crucial was clear to everyone, but they were not the only matters to be dealt with. Mr. Dahl also foresaw some other problems coming up:

"Do you realize high taxes are here and apt to stay, and is your business geared accordingly?" he went on. "Some of the answers to the questions I have asked can be found through collective action—through our trade associations—national, state and local. We know that one of these days soon competition will again become keen; certainly we do not want ruinous price cutting to be our only answer.

"A moving service, be it long distance or local, cannot be sold in the usual manner. It is hard to visualize the type of advertising, publicity or salesmanship that would make a person want to move the same way you can make a person want to own a new automobile, suit of clothes, home or refrigerator. A person usually moves because he has to. The proper time, therefore, to put across our story is when people are interested in our product. Today, almost anyone might be faced with a moving problem in the immediate future. When so many thousands are interested in moving and storage, this is the time to tell our story. . . . Let's tell what we are doing to help win the War. That we are and will continue to serve the public to the best of our ability. . . . That we are giving 100% more service with less men and less equipment. . . . That we look to the day when we can again render 'Service as Usual. . . .'"

Many of the thoughts that Dahl expressed at that time, more than 25 years ago, show how he and others were troubled about the days ahead. Others were not as aware of their problems and opportunities and were left by the wayside, especially in terms of being able to sell their services in a fresh way, when people no longer *had* to accept just that service that they could get.

The War was far from won when Dahl made his speech, but its outcome was becoming more clear to the average citizen. The ability to produce and transport things and people was beginning to pay off for the Allies, perhaps as much as, if not more than, their fighting ability.

The industry's participation had many touching and dramatic moments, where lives were actually saved as a result of a mover's work. In fact, many a fallen American airplane was helped directly by the Lyon Van and Storage Company operation in Los Angeles, where Lyon's trained crew moved in and salvaged the plane, putting in force its knowledge about this highly specialized business with a speed that had been perfected by its long experience in doing a kind of work unique to the field.

Because of its knowledge of disassembling, packing, crating, and shipping planes, the job of salvaging naturally fell to Lyon's aeronautical division. Since planes have a way of going down far from civilization and from organized, "regular" roads, the Lyon crews often had to show their own kind of bravery to match that of the fallen pilot. When a call was received that a plane was down, a Lyon surveyor was dispatched to the scene of the crash. He photographed the wreckage and made an inventory of all equipment and plane parts damaged. He also surveyed the available roads where a crew might get to the scene of the accident. Thus, he could recommend the kind of hauling equipment that might best travel over the often difficult roads of a usual crash area.

Some special security precautions were necessary: first, all secret equipment and all casualties were taken out before the Lyon specialists were allowed to view the scene. Then, the special equipment and crew were sent in. On one occasion, it took 14 hours for the Lyon crew to go through 2 miles of unusually tough terrain to reach the scene of the crash. In many cases, a private farmer's field had to be crossed and the surveyor, often using the skill of a master salesman, had to arrange for special payment of right-of-way.

Many unpleasant scenes were met by the Lyon man when he arrived at a crash, but he was involved. He helped directly with the War effort, as much as any man in a rescue squadron did.

There were other ways, too, that industry was drawn into the War effort, occasionally humorously, but often to the exasperation of anyone trying to do business as usual. At times, household-goods shipments would be stalled in midpassage. And very frequently the occasion was caused by faulty tires — but who needed them more than a mover? In September, 1944, The Household Goods Carriers Conference of the American Trucking Association asked the War Production Board for a 2-A priority for heavy-duty tires. This category, for some reason, was not given to the moving and storage people but it was to intercity truck lines. Household goods were given the rating of Group #3. The complaints were coming in from all parts of the country, and from important operators.

Very briefly, here are some of the complaints in the words of the men involved, which show as much as anything both the pride and the frustration of trying to do a job with less than perfect equipment: "We already have seven loaded vans stopped," said E. S. Wheaton, Aero-Mayflower Transit Co., Indianapolis. "Our emergency reserve is entirely exhausted. More than 100 vans now are operating without a spare. . . ." Lee J. Sloan, president at the time, of United Van Lines. . . . "We have no new tires on hand. . . ." "Delay of two to five days with vans loaded with Army personnel effects," reported Merle Fullerton, President, North American Van Lines. . . . "These movements originated from Washington and Cincinnati—and with Navy personnel goods out of Chicago and Camp Lee. We have no stock tires on hand and only ten tires that are now recapped. Twenty percent of our fleet are running without spares. . . ."

One wonders what happened to both the people and the goods on the road on dark nights when the tires ran out and there were no spares? Things just sat and the red tape rolled on. It was indeed a tough time to do business.

As in so many cases before, however, this country coped with its transportation and supply problems. New organizations and new energies growing out of the War's special demands were being created. In 1943, the American Movers Conference was organized and then was reorganized in 1944. Incorporated in 1947 under the laws of the District of Columbia, it changed its name in 1951 from Household Goods Carriers Conference to American Movers Conference (AMC).

These beginnings, coming out of the Second World War, have led it to a membership of more than 2,000 individual carriers—local, intrastate, and interstate, along with a number of Canadian members and several in Asia, Europe, and South America.

Long before that busy time, the Household Goods Carriers Bureau, the Movers and Warehousemen's Association of America, Inc., and the Mayflower Warehousemen's Association had begun to share a role with the NFWA in the industry's behalf, showing their interest in upgrading the profession and in telling the real story of the moving man to the general public.

Even the British, who had gone through so much, could turn

their eyes forward and see a light at the end of their long, tortuous tunnel. A British trade association, The National Association of Furniture Warehousemen and Removers, Ltd., commented in 1944: "We write at a moment when things are happening fast. After long waiting, after months of slogging work, without respite or rest, our hopes are raised and we are keyed up to great expectations."

The English observer, with these hopeful expectations, was optimistic, however, in a typical British, understated way: "Will the end come during the next few weeks or will it be many months? It does not matter—we have a glimpse of the end of the road, and that is sufficient to inspire us to tackle the last lap or so with renewed energy. . . . We write from a target area. During the day, possibly we have now and again swiftly wondered if we should put the telephone down and dive for cover; and now at home, there is the same intermittent alert. It is not very conducive to concentration. In the meantime we idly turn over the pages of *Removals and Storage.* These pages, seven or eight years old, which we turn, curiously enough, contain some of our post-war problems . . . unsolved and pigeon-holed. They must one day be faced."

This British operator had been under the gun directly for many years and was vulnerable to destruction. Damage could not only wipe out operations for several days, but could eliminate everything for all time. But he could still comment about the problems, stated in the industry journals of 1938. They were unsolved, just as they were in America. . . .

"There are, for example, our shelved transport rates structure and the standardization and cooperative purchase of motor vehicles and plant. A paper written for a conference in Chester in 1936 carried problems that might be written for 1945!"

Nothing had been done, although the changes in the British economy had been enormous. The same situation, sadly enough, held true in this country. Only the physical pain and the bombing had been absent. The reports coming, however, were almost as painful to read as to live through.

Meanwhile, other reports coming into this country from moving and storage people in other parts of the battered world were not happy ones, either. C. A. Aspinwall, President of Security Storage Company in Washington, D.C., attested to the many and varied responses he had received about other storage and moving men around the world: From Poland: "Mr. Josef Obojoki, assistant manager of Wroblewski's moving firm, Warsaw, states that the Wroblewski family's whereabouts are completely unknown. Their property is considered abandoned and is being managed by the Warsaw municipal administration. . . . The firm's offices were destroyed and the building is in ruins, the rolling stock was taken by the Germans and only four undamaged warehouses are left. . . ."

From Manila, the Philippines: "The Luzon Brokerage Company reopened its office on July 20, 1945, in one room of the Derham Building. . . . All of the rest of the building is occupied by the U.S. Army. . . . We started from scratch. All of our records were destroyed or otherwise disposed of by the Imperial Japanese Army. We have not even a piece of paper three inches square—no office equipment, no garage equipment, all our trucks were turned over to the U.S. Army on December 8, 1941. . . ."

This correspondent dropped from 169 pounds at the start of his captivity in a Japanese prison camp to about 98 pounds at the time of his liberation. From Europe, from Asia, from all over, the theme was the same: terrible things have happened. What do we do to recover?

Although moving and storage operators in this country were not physically affected by bombing and enemy occupation, for example, they were often going through radical changes as a result of their relationship to the federal government.

In January, 1944, the Department of Justice filed an antitrust suit against the NFWA and charged the Association with discriminatory practices, and sought to compel the NFWA to divest itself of any and all interest in Allied Van Lines. A short time later, the Association voted to divest itself of the Allied stock on a voluntary basis by adoption of the following resolution:

"This Board of Directors denies there has been any violation of the anti-trust laws by NFWA or by Allied. Nevertheless, to avoid unnecessary litigation with the United States government in time of war, it deems it desirable and for the best interest of NFWA and the membership thereof that NFWA divest itself of all stock interest in Allied and completely divorce the activities of NFWA from the operation, management or control of Allied."

In 1946, the Interstate Commerce Commission authorized Allied Van Lines, Inc., to purchase the operating rights of more than 400 carriers, and by the end of 1946 the industry was represented by an independent association.

The boom arising from the return of servicemen called for greater service and mobility. Shifts in population from the East to the West, from the South to the Northern urban centers, from home town to bustling city—all have been mentioned and would be increasingly important in the years ahead.

The old problem came up again—the inability of obtaining return loads in order to fully utilize personnel and equipment. It was necessary for firms to cooperate again to get their jobs done.

Throughout the Americas, where no great physical damage was done to plant or people, still the War had its effect . . . in a variety of places.

Western Cartage and Storage, Inc., of Edmonton, Canada, for instance, saw tremendous changes in their operation. They learned the new technology, especially in the transport of aircraft engines, and they rushed loads daily to aircraft bound for the Alaskan Highway. Unlike many moving companies, they had the inclination to put all this experience into a handsome booklet that might well serve any industry history. The pamphlet is called "A Moving Story." It is.

Many changes were taking place in the continental United States, too. Sometime after the War, Lyon Van and Storage

Company actually converted a World War II War plant in San Diego, California, to a warehouse that afforded many labor-saving devices, introduced highly improved housekeeping measures, and combined storage in the commercial and furniture areas that effected great savings for these two functions that, before this time, had seemed so incompatible.

Vans entered huge former hangar doors, which were apart from the commercial section, while household goods were taken to the mezzanine. Commercial storage entered through another section and the business was carried on as two separate but related functions—unheard of before in most operations—under one roof. The experiment seemed to make the best of two heretofore different worlds.

Also, many industry leaders published papers and gave talks before conventions about the future of air transportation of household goods. Since so many members of NFWA had taken part in this kind of work during the War, it was the general feeling that the plans for air transportation were inevitably going to have to be coped with, but that the short-range feasibility for profitable air handling would be slight. Costs just seemed too high; in fact, they still do in many areas of the country. But the assessments were interesting and showed how people were trying to plan for the postwar expansion that many observers saw as imposing its own kind of completely new reality on the business.

Before these future plans could be carefully considered, however, a series of incidents in the mid-forties caused everyone to wonder if the whole world was completely out of control.

On April 13, 1945, Franklin Roosevelt suddenly died of a cerebral hemorrhage, so suddenly, in fact, that he could not even be transferred to his bed before he was dead.

On April 30, as the Russians raged outside his bunker, Adolf Hitler killed himself, along with his mistress, Eva Braun.

On July 5, the British held a general election which was to eventually remove its great wartime leader, Winston Churchill, from public office. When the returns were finally counted,

Mr. Churchill was forced to withdraw from the crucial Potsdam Conference attended by Josef Stalin and our new President, Harry Truman.

On August 6, the atomic bomb was dropped on a previously obscure Japanese town called Hiroshima, killing 60,175 human beings. On August 9, another bomb was dropped on Nagasaki, Japan, killing approximately 30,000 people and injuring about 60,000 more.

On August 16, the Japanese surrendered on the deck of the battleship *Missouri*. A new age was upon us.

Soon, the moving and storage business would be taking for granted the American corporate move and the standing Army that still moved huge quantities of men, materials, and household goods.

"Following the War, the stationing of large military forces overseas," said David Brodsky, "produced a dramatic impact on the whole business of shipping household goods. An entirely new field of business was opened to the moving industry. The decision to have Mrs. GI Joe join her husband overseas and establish a reasonable facsimile of her American home abroad had a revolutionary effect on the industry. A new kind of service was established: Motor Van–Sea Van service, in which steel containers were packed with the householder's goods and consigned to a port agent in the country where the serviceman was to be stationed. This kind of worldwide service, made necessary by the ever-present American serviceman and the postwar extension of the operators of American corporations and multinational corporations seeking new and expanding markets in all parts of the world, opened up great new opportunities for those who could take advantage of them."

Americans would expect to travel fast and effortlessly over the new superhighways of the next decade, their household goods following right behind them. Often these same people would also be establishing "second homes" (a growing trend), on the way to unprecedented affluence.

Many warehouses, van lines, and even some newly organized

firms previously unaffiliated with the moving and storage industry participated in the phase of moving activity as forwarders of used household goods and soon formed a new organization—The Household Goods Forwarders Association of America—to handle common problems and protect their common interests.

For the moving and storage industry, the War was to present two very special opportunities, in the areas of people to be served and in the special innovations arising out of the urgent needs of a nation fighting a war on a worldwide scale.

In 1940, in "Northern America" as the population experts described America and Canada, to differentiate from Latin America, the population was approximately 144 million people. By 1950, however, the population had increased to 166 million people, despite the most destructive war the world had ever seen.

After World War II ended, the increase in this country's population was enormous. The effects of this so-called "baby boom" were to prove immense. For example, most American children are born to women between the ages of 20 to 29. Women of this important age group will have increased by 35% between 1968 and 1975. Therefore, these children born after the War are now reaching their maximum reproductive years. There are simply more "producers" of children, no matter how effective birth control and other factors may prove to be in American society.

For instance, people who are most prone to move are approximately in the 25- to 32-year-old age group. The "baby boom" which began in 1945, the year that the War ended, contributed to a total North American population of 233 million people in 1970. Thus the moving and storage industry has already been faced and will continue to be faced with enormous challenges in moving these additional people who are the most mobile in our society.

Also, as is commonly known, World War II produced many innovations, inventions, and new products which affected all of American society, and especially the moving and storage industry. For example, nylon, the "walkie talkie," foam rubber, and many other new materials changed the materials handling, communications, and storage elements of the industry. For instance, the "walkie talkie" was the communications foundation for the present instant communications system that is now available between the moving van and the dispatcher; ropes and tie-down equipment are nylon; many of the packaging products are synthetic material; and new packaging techniques have been made possible through the development of these materials which are a far cry from the old sugar barrel or tea box and excelsior days. The composition of numerous household items was changed by the invention of foam rubber, plastics, and other synthetic materials which required new handling techniques and methods of protection.

Early days . . . *(Also see following spread)*

Historic moves. *Until the nineteen forties, the moving of the Hughes flying boat from Culver City to Long Beach, California, was the biggest single moving operation in history. (Left) Truck rounding a corner with the 160-foot wing section. (Left, below) The fuselage section of the flying boat, as large as an ordinary dirigible, cradled on rolling dollies.*

Moving the world's largest oil painting, Pantheon de la Guerre by Pierre Carrier-Belleuse, for the Golden Gate Exposition— April, 1940.

PANTHEON DE LA GUERRE---THE WORLD'S LARGEST OIL PAINTING
THE LARGEST SINGLE PACKAGE TO BE STORED IN A WAREHOUSE
55 FEET LONG-8 FEET WIDE-8 FEET HIGH---VALUE $100,000.00
STORED BY DAVIDSON FOR 8 YEARS
LOADED-HAULED-BRACED ON SPECIAL FREIGHT CAR
FOR GOLDEN GATE EXPOSITION-APRIL 29,1940.

NO.1055

Moving and storage today. (Left) *Air to ground transport of goods.* (Above) *Ground to ship transport.*

A Boeing 707-321C all-cargo jet freighter about to be loaded for overseas delivery.

Transporting goods by ship.

America on the move . . . (Above) *Office moving.* (Right, above) *Mobile telephones on today's vans enable drivers to keep in contact with dispatcher and customer.* (Right, below) *Equipment being moved into a maternity ward.*

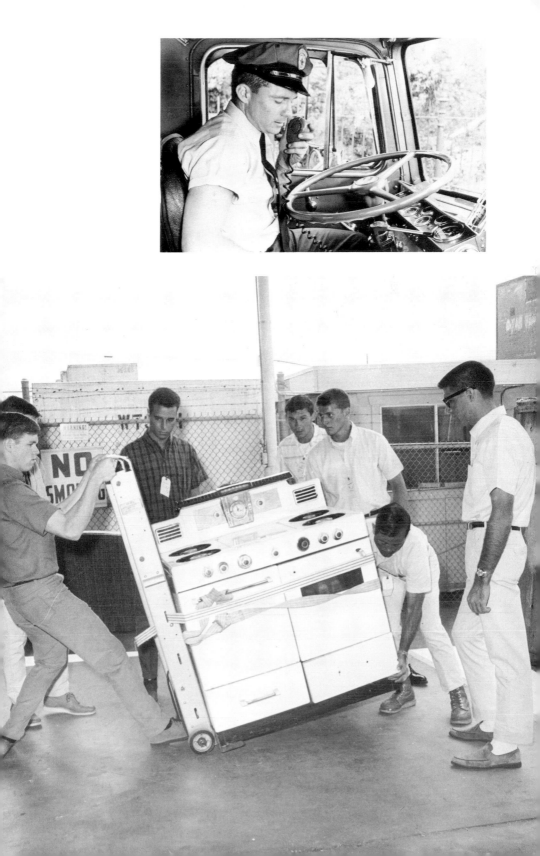

Transporting a jungle friend.

Computer sections being moved from a plane on a forklift.

Moving "the world's largest frying pan."

Today's storage techniques. (Above) *Specially designed pallet boxes used to store davenports and armchairs. (Also see overleaf)*

*Diagonal bracing, overlapping joints, and corner
battens extending to the floor contribute to the
strength of this box.*

5

The Quiet, Fat Fifties

The 1940's ended in a blaze of activity around the world. The entire fabric of the civilized world had been changed by the biggest War in history, changed for all time in geography and in mores, in living habits and in the levels of affluence that were now available, especially to the American worker.

At the end of 1949, Mainland China fell to Communist forces who picked an auspicious date to drive Nationalist forces from the country: It was eight years to the day after Pearl Harbor.

The world's moving habits were changing as never before. Corporations were now rich enough and daring enough that they were willing to subsidize the move of a man and his household furniture from Milwaukee to New York, from Des Moines to Phoenix, from Tucson to Hong Kong—if the organization thought the move would produce profit from this investment.

On June 27, 1950, the United Nations Security Council voted to assist South Korea with all necessary means, in their struggle to resist the North Korean Army that had invaded the south with 60,000 troops and a spearhead of 100 Russian-built tanks. War had again made it necessary to ship men and their possessions overseas on a grand scale. On that same day in June, President Harry Truman ordered General Douglas MacArthur to Korea as Commander of UN troops there.

Also, the military situation was just an adjunct to the corporate moves that were to become so commonplace to so many men and their families. This combination of factors brought more business and more challenges for moving companies throughout the country. And so it was inevitable that in the 1950's the American woman entered the action, mostly as counterego to her rising young husband who was moving up and around in the corporation. She was the person on the spot at both the beginning and the end of the journey, the lady whom the moving company had to deal with, placate, satisfy, and hope to move again.

It is worthwhile to quote from one of the most important books published during those days, one that is still read for general edification and, also, by business school graduates. It is William Whyte's *The Organization Man,* which came out in a very important year, 1956. The book sets a tone and talks about the commitment that the American woman, especially the educated American woman, had made to take her place beside her husband in business now that he had returned from war. *The New York Times* said at the time of the book's appearance: "Most wives agreed with the corporation; they too felt that the good wife is the wife who adjusts graciously to the system, curbs open intellectualism or the desire to be alone. . . . A frequent consequence is the 'superwoman' complex. . . . They take on a backbreaking load of duties, and a feeling of guilt that they're not up to it. . . ."

In this very commitment to the life of her husband and the corporation that Whyte talks about, we see a direct relationship on the part of the corporate woman with the willingness to move, to try new places, to better her economic condition. She was destined to move much more than her mother—and thus be the person most involved with the moving company. This corporate wife would have the education and capability to expect the moving man to be more professional, more considerate, and more efficient than her counterpart, who might have moved during the worst times of the Depression from one cold-water flat back to her family home with her husband and children in order to recuperate from business failures. She simply expected more now.

The moving estimator and manager were now dealing with sophisticated people in a wide range of situations. These moving men were also coming to grips with the corporation traffic manager who was concerned on a number of levels with the performance of the individual mover, in a much more exacting manner than the COD family. Why? His job depended on how well his overall costs could be measured against his company budget, how efficiently his fellow employees, from the president of the company to the newest business school graduate, could be most satisfactorily moved from one place to another. The traffic manager had to engage, in many case, a company that could move very complicated equipment, large and small, from highly technical space gear to the largest computer — the most expensive that giants like International Business Machines, for example, owned. He had to answer, too, when things went wrong within his company, and answers for *his* questions had to come instantly and comprehensively from the moving and storage expert who handled the individual assignment.

Up to this point in history, business conditions had changed considerably as Americans attempted to adjust to the 1950's. Added to this was the decision that President Eisenhower made in 1954, one that has permanently altered the face of this nation, and has radically affected the flow of truck and car traffic from one end of the country to another. This was the famous National System of Interstate and Defense Highways, whose red, white, and blue shields are now familiar guideposts to millions of American motorists — and to millions of consumers who have watched their personal possessions move across these same highways. There is no question that the highway system has revolutionized both the mode and the quantity of long-distance American travel and general mobility.

"Before concrete"—a chapter title for this book, incidentally, suggested by a prominent member of the moving and storage industry—roads were messy, uneven, and just plain bad. In the 1930's, for example, there were still big problems, as anyone ever following a heavily laden truck up a hill through a rainstorm in rural Iowa can attest to. When the Interstate System of four-lane, high-speed travel was proposed and furthermore made into reality, the moving business really was given an opportunity for a giant step forward.

Soon it would be possible to bypass cities completely, to drive or to move goods, in most cases with highway safety checks, through the country without stopping for a traffic light. Spurs from cities would connect with the Interstate System and there would be no massive backups and delays as had happened before under the best of conditions.

Highway plans made in the 1950's were, of course, often idealistic. Things did not work out simply or neatly much of the time, especially for the mover. But he still moved faster and better, with the corporate mover right there with him.

The original Eisenhower proposal was to be financed through a Highway Trust Fund—in which all federal taxes on motor vehicles, gasoline, oil, and ancillary equipment would be channeled into this fund and devoted entirely to highway construction.

The federal government would pay for 90% of the construction of interstate projects; states would collect their own automobile and truck taxes and would pay the remaining 10%. The 1956 Highway Act provided that public hearings should be held whenever an interstate road was planned to by-pass or run right through a community. These public hearings had a large effect on the way the roads were finally laid out. However, costs got so out of hand that the original estimated cost of the Interstate System of $27 billion had grown by 1966, just ten years later, to $46.8 billion.

Still, the effects that the System had on the moving and storage industry and its freedom to move more goods at a faster rate are, in the opinion of many experts, the most important events of the 1950's. Immediately a Westward movement began once more, as well as a South-to-North exodus that would have made the pioneers gasp with admiration. Also, individuals moved to the city as never before, both as private persons and in family groups.

The effects that the Interstate System has already had on the moving and storage business are gigantic. Eventually, the Interstate System will connect and serve 90% of all cities of over 50,000 population . . . and many smaller cities and towns. As of 1971, however, the cost of the system will be approximately $70 billion, while by time of completion economic benefits to users are expected to total $107 billion as of latest projections received from the United States Department of Transportation.

In the preservation of human life alone, present figures supplied by the U.S. Transportation Department, Federal Highway Administration, predict a reduction in highway deaths of as many as 8,000 a year. The economic growth created along the interstate highways is bound to be impressive, for about 85% of the Interstate System is being built on entirely new location, creating new opportunities for business development in those areas of the country not previously served by the System.

Such wholesale moving, caused by these factors of expansion of roads, increased corporate activity and transfers, and the general restlessness of an already chronically restless nation, caused enormous problems—and opportunities. The amount of change and challenge can be dramatically measured by one stark statistic: since the inception of the Interstate Highway Fund of 1956, a total of $195 billion has been spent on all highways, and only $32 billion on all other forms of transportation. Cars and trucks—the amateur and the professional mover—were remaking the face of America.

To capitalize on this increased activity and the challenges of dealing with a "different" kind of customer in many cases, the

NFWA engaged in an imaginative and far-seeing plan to up-grade the professionalism of the industry and to ensure for other areas of growth if the industry were to prosper and, indeed, if it were to survive at all.

This program was called The Master Plan of Expansion, and J. C. Aspinwall, Jr., President of NFWA at the time, summarized the essential parts of the Plan as follows:

"As a result of a series of conferences between industry leaders, general agreement was reached that the grave problems facing our industry could be segregated into several general areas: *1. A general lack of standard operating procedures; 2. The need for scientific accuracy in care and handling of modern materials and fabrics; 3. The need to attract to our industry bright young men capable of assuming future leadership.*"

To deal with these problems, Mr. Aspinwall proposed that a threefold program taking in research, education and training be adopted. A vehicle for funding such projects would be created through a "not-for-profit corporation" whose name would be *The National Moving and Storage Technical Foundation.* The Foundation was to be governed by a Board of Trustees made up of leading members of the industry, allied industries, and the general public. Three phases of activity were planned for the first year: 1. Establishment of a field engineering service. 2. Establishment of a scientific program of research benefiting all segments of the industry and the general public. 3. Establishment of a technical education course at a university devoted to scientific research.

The engineers were to bring to the individual companies in the field the benefit of technical, scientific information procured from research and study carried on by the research of the Technical Foundation.

At that time, Mr. Aspinwall continued, there was a general lack of knowledge about the physical characteristics and limitations of certain key physical products that the members were constantly using. This program of solving these particular problems was to be carried on by an independent educational institution, one previously specializing in similar research and testing activities for other industries.

The Technical Foundation was also able to work out the establishment of an accounting manual, a management tool that would create uniformity in accounting procedures and management techniques. The need to establish this system of knowing real costs has been, perhaps, one of the most pressing industrywide problems over the years. The industry, because of its special operating procedures, has had considerable problems in knowing and controlling *its actual costs*.

Eventually, the accounting manual involved the talents of Price Waterhouse & Company and the staff of the NFWA in order to produce a flexible accounting plan for companies of all sizes. It was recognized that this special kind of business included all kinds of firms, of various operating techniques, in every part of the country. The accounting manual produced a program for controlling costs and for planning that had not existed before.

Several of the important advantages which were proposed as being possible to accomplish at that time were: A reduction in claims; the substitution of scientifically accurate methods for the currently popular device of solving each crisis as it came along with no systematic planning; and the availability of reliable, authentic data for the field engineer to pass on to industry members whom they contacted.

Mr. Aspinwall went on to describe one area that was crucial to the survival of the business: the ability to plan ahead and to anticipate problems before they had formed and had become so huge that they were largely insoluble. It was this fault, Aspinwall felt, that caused the industry to be so generally shy of true management potential, including young men who could be expected to grow as the years progressed, as well as seasoned professionals thoroughly grounded in their field.

Through a technical education course, professionally training men to take their places in the industry (and administered by a technical university), the Foundation would gradually furnish this group of men so desperately needed. The eventual result of this reservoir of talent would be beneficial, and would enhance the image of an industry in the eyes of the general public which would quickly welcome the raising of standards and performance by the men that it dealt with.

The plan made absolutely good sense. It would help to unify a trouble-filled industry that was trying very hard at the time to break away from the bonds that had limited its growth, when compared with other transportation forms. Of course, general industry as well had grown at a fantastic clip since the end of the War. "The Foundation would help the moving and storage industry take its proper place in the nation's economy," Mr. Aspinwall said.

About a month after this "revolutionary" doctrine was announced, Donald R. Markham, then executive director of the Foundation, expanded on Mr. Aspinwall's thoughts after they had been given at the Hotel del Coronado in Coronado, California. Commenting principally on the first two of the three main Foundation objectives, Mr. Markham announced the leadership which was to guide the Foundation. Representatives from the industry were: Chairman George Winkler, Jr., Chester E. Bradley, Herbert B. Holt, Marion W. Niedringhaus, Jerome D. Ullman, and J. C. Aspinwall, Jr. Public trustees named were: John K. Gund, President, United Van Lines; an officer still to be named from the First National Bank of Chicago, and an officer from the famous Armour Research Foundation of Illinois Institute of Technology.

Three projects had been immediately started with the research facility at the Armour Research Foundation. Because of many reports detailing serious problems encountered in the storage and handling of the newer type of *fabric* at this time, that particular project was put at the top of the list. The importance of scientific evaluation of the handling of synthetic materials was an important factor in this decision. For example, if the Foundation in its research found that foam rubber, because of its physical characteristics, must be stored in a certain way and within prescribed limitations of both temperature and humidity, a serious claim problem in the industry could be reduced, if not eliminated completely, from daily activities.

Once this specialized information was readily available, Mr. Markham pointed out, the next problem was to communicate it to the industry. Before, the method of printed information, in not always easy-to-read form, had proved to be inadequate — and largely unsuccessful. Now, the field engineer, with his on-the-spot presence, could communicate his message directly and actively to the men in the field. The selection of highly trained men with an ability to both analyze and summarize a problem clearly and concisely was paramount. The recruiting of quality men, then, was the first order of business.

In addition, the field engineers were to do more than merely report recent research findings. They were to encompass the entire sphere of industrywide education — and pass this education along to the operator in the field. As many as 16 subjects were listed in the original training brochure.

Overall, the game plan was to eliminate flying by the seat of the pants, a situation where industry might simply be putting out a small fire only to let a larger one simmer and grow larger as time went on. The third phase of working with the technical schools was deferred until the second year of the Technical Foundation's existence.

This kind of operation took money, which became quickly available. Substantial sums had been made available by sources outside the industry, and some services were supplied free of charge in lieu of a cash grant. This vote of confidence, Markham felt, indicated that the industry was improving its role in the national economy, and also showed the vision of certain leaders in allied industries who would benefit by an elevation of professional standards.

The Fireman's Fund Insurance Company made the charter contribution with which the Technical Foundation was founded. Overall, Markham saw the industry's previous growth from "its humble beginnings" to a key place in the volatile economy of the time.

There were probably not many people around in those days who would have not recognized the special problem, however. Now, the struggle could be *effective* and *united*.

However, there was not always only grim reality to cope with in those days of fantastic growth for the economy and the industry. No matter how effective and complex an organization might be, it is simply composed of people, as infinitely complex and interesting as any organization chart can be. An important man in industry who represented both early beginnings and the most modern of adjustments to current business activity was Louis Schramm, Jr., who was honored at a testimonial dinner at the Waldorf Astoria where more than 500 people from across the country accepted invitations to honor the President of Chelsea Warehouses, Inc., New York City, and also the President of Allied Van Lines, Inc. Mr. Schramm was given a sterling silver plaque by the NFWA in "recognition of his unselfish devotion to the problems of the warehousing industry." Like so many formal inscriptions, this statement told only the surface story of an enormous contribution.

Many other long-time friends attending the dinner must have smiled wisely to themselves as Mr. Schramm rose to accept this tribute. One who was there remembers with delight earlier occasions where Mr. Schramm performed his many contributions to the industry.

"Louis Schramm was a giant among other men in the industry," Brodsky said recently. "He was a product of the New York streets, but had enough personality and talent to hold any job, at any level, both in public life or in the professions. He was an activist. His father happened to be in the warehouse business on 26th Street in New York City, so Louis spent much of his early life literally hanging around the horse barn. His father felt that his son needed some strict discipline in order to mold his character in the correct manner, so he sent Louis to a military academy. This seemed fitting and proper to Mr. Schramm, Sr., who was by nature a strict disciplinarian and a believer in order, above all, especially for young people.

"When he finished the military academy, Louis rebelled even more against this strong-willed father whom he loved but still refused to obey. He would not go into the family business at that time. Instead, he stayed in the warehouse business — but on his own. He bought a warehouse in Bronxville, which was called the Gramaton Storage Company. He was in his early years then and eager to show his dominant father that he could make good on his own. . . . His first venture in the business happened to be very successful. Louis was a man who would take a chance on his ability to capitalize on a given situation. He was a 'quick study' and moved rapidly in business operations.

"Ironically, when the Depression hit New York, Louis, Jr., was in a position to help his own father out of difficulties that the family business had fallen into. However, neither the younger nor the elder Schramm got along with a partner and relative, Fred Hahn. Louis, Jr., laid down the law: he would come in and help bail out his father if Mr. Hahn got out. This was arranged shortly thereafter, but feelings remained bad and this arrangement laid the basis for a family feud that went on for years. However, with typical energy and activism, Louis got the family business back on its feet; later the Chelsea name became a landmark in the New York business world."

There was a deep relationship, too, between Louis and Charley Morgan, or C. D., as he was known, another giant in the Eastern moving and storage parade. Schramm's friend of those years goes on:

"In the darkest days of the Depression, C. D. Morgan had his main operation on 21st Street. . . . The backgrounds of both C. D. Morgan and Louis Schramm were quite different, although they were the best of friends. Previous to this relationship, Charley's father and Louis's father were also good friends, but C. D.'s father's appearance was natty to say the least—and he often arrived at his place of business in a hansom cab, brandishing a silver-headed cane with all the trimmings of the time. But later conditions changed drastically for both families, as they did with many people. Through both prosperous and hard times, the two families stuck together as friends, but especially C. D. and Louis, Jr., remained close.

"It is my opinion," said David Brodsky, "that Louis set the pace of business decisions and used foresight, and C. D. did, also. . . . As the industry developed, Louis was called upon frequently for public speaking assignments, and he quickly became a gifted speaker. He gained a following in the New York area first, but he also was proficient enough to attract a number of interested admirers throughout the country. When Allied started up operations, Louis became quite involved and interested in its total operation, and this activity laid the foundation for his later assuming the presidency of Allied Van Lines. He gave his support to Martin Kennelly and Tony Cresto, a well-known Kansas City moving company executive, who were older, and of course Martin was the chief organizer of Allied in those early days. . . . Louis did much of the 'leg work' actually when Allied was first getting off the ground.

"After Kennelly entered Chicago politics, later to be mayor of that city, Louis continued his strong interest in Allied. He was the logical choice to be named president later. In fact, in the opinion of many, he was the most effective president up to that time, and his administration ushered in the golden period of Allied's activity. He developed and established its leadership and managed its often painful growth under the government regulations that Allied had to deal with considering the new laws of the times. These harrowing experiences are well-known to everyone in the business."

The same eyewitness to those Waldorf festivities knew Louis Schramm as well as anyone and has contributed numerous anecdotes that show the effects that this dynamic leader had on his industry and his times:

"C. D. Morgan and Louis Schramm were indeed giants in every sense of the term. However, they had a basic falling out that affected the industry, especially in New York, and which is important to the general history of those times. The incident centered on the selection of the Impartial Chairman of New York City, a special post dedicated to solving disputes between consumer and moving company. Louis was against one man, while Morgan felt strongly that Louis was being patently unfair to this man, who he felt could make a real contribution toward solving the moving and storage problems of New York. No matter what happened about this particular man (and I truly do not remember what did happen to him) the friendship between these two titans was permanently damaged. It just goes to show how strongly and how responsibly these two men could feel about their business lives. It was sad to see it happen —and as I said—the relationship was never the same after that."

While these very events were taking place at the Waldorf, many other situations, both favorable and unfavorable, were taking shape in the world outside those venerable halls.

A few years before the meeting in New York honoring Schramm, the steel industry's labor unions had decided they had a war to wage of their own during the Korean conflict and embarked on one of the longest and costliest strikes ever in that all-important industry.

The effects were felt in every segment of the economy. Even though President Eisenhower was successful in fulfilling his campaign pledge to end the Korean War, the technological changes that were affecting American business — automation, containerization, labor problems, continuing inflation — were still considered minor when compared to the dreaded, often frightening effects of the Cold War and the Russian-Chinese alliance that both scared and angered many average Americans.

Shortly before the dinner at the Waldorf, Senator Joseph McCarthy had fascinated and eventually repelled the nation with his antics on television—particularly during the Army-McCarthy trials. The good sense of the American people prevailed, however, and McCarthy was formally rebuked by his colleagues in the Senate, and later died in relative obscurity.

There were many forces at play in the economy at this time, but especially these two factors: the influence of the corporation on American life and the pervading and subtle relationship that we held with Russia, constituting the Cold War psychology which became even more of a household word after Korea had been "settled." Both forces had decided effects on the moving and storage industry.

In the corporate sector, one shipper who controlled a great deal of business and was articulate in expressing what was wanted from a mover was the General Foods Corporation. In 1956, GF's traffic manager, Robert E. Fox, delivered an address that is both indicative of the times and of the industry's "big shipper" who with his repeat business was and is a crucial man to please.

"Since we try to select a carrier with strong representation in both the origin and destination city," Mr. Fox began, "if the employee has moved before, and if his last move has been handled satisfactorily by the carrier selected, and if this carrier has good agents at either end of the new move, then the booking will be made in his favor.

"If the employee's previous move has been unsatisfactory from either a service or a claim point of view, we will select a different carrier for the new move. Allocation of our total volume of business among the carriers used by General Foods is also an important consideration, but not an overriding one."

In clear and simple terms, Mr. Fox went on to spell out what he expected from the moving industry. "General Foods' requirements of the movers with whom we do business are numerous and in some cases exacting, but they are not unreasonable, in our opinion. We require the mover to be strongly represented at both origin and destination city or reasonably close to the two points. Since many of our moves require storage in transit until the employee is to report to the new job by a particular date, the ability to be able to depend on the accuracy of estimated dates of arrival and departure is crucial. . . ."

So few words tell it all: When can you be there, what can you produce, and who will be on the other end? Mr. Fox and his companions are used to wholesale moves, as anyone living in Westchester County, New York, in the late 1950's will attest to. GF moved from Manhattan to a suburban location in White Plains, New York, one of the first important moves away from the often painful method of doing business in Manhattan.

Mr. Fox stated further General Foods' expectations:

"We would much prefer that a carrier tell us in advance that he cannot handle a move rather than to accept the booking and then not be able to fulfill the schedule required. A carrier does *not* jeopardize his participation in our business if he frankly says that he can't handle a move because he is all booked up, or because he does not think that his agent at destination or origin point is capable of properly servicing the move. . . . The allocation of our shipments is deliberately set up to perment flexibility of choice in the selection of a carrier, so we are not really being inconvenienced when a mover advises he can't take on a particular booking. . . ."

General Foods moved a great many people in the 1950's, and their patterns of doing business, along with those of International Business Machines Company and other large companies, determined much of what the industry reacted to in the corporate sector.

Again, Fox frankly referred to his company's requirements:

"Each national account has laid down its own ground rules for its employees to be governed by, whenever transfer of household effects is involved. All of our carriers are required to be familiar with these limitations so that the corporate interest will be protected."

In closing, Fox also made some apt comments about the newly hired graduate of a college or university, and how this situation would leave its mark on the 1950's and the moving and storage industry:

"The hiring of college graduates has increased the activity

of national movers a great deal. Often, these kinds of moves would closely resemble a nuisance move. They often originate in some remote campus location where moving volume is normally low. They frequently represent little revenue to the mover, since the new employee and his possessions are usually limited to a chair or two, a trunk, possibly a desk and usually and often a TV set, hi-fi, or both. Looking at it from our side of the fence, it is just as important for this man to be moved efficiently and quickly as it is for a senior executive with many more expensive possessions who has 'arrived' in our business. The reasons are clear: it is from these junior executives that industry expects to develop the leaders of tomorrow, those men who will be asked to do the most and will, therefore, be moving the most in the years ahead. They remember well; that's why we think they will be leaders. And they will surely remember those moving companies who give them good service early on in their careers."

One other social phenomenon of those years, in addition to the influence of the corporate sector, was the special quality of the "Cold War." Indeed, at that time there was genuine fear about atomic attack, as there is sometimes today, in a much different way. But who can ever forget the run on bomb shelers of the late 1950's and early 1960's? The headlines in the *Saturday Evening Post* about how to protect your family against raining H-bombs were phenomena of those days.

One of the most famous hospitals in the country, one enjoying an extremely high professional rating, is Massachusetts General Hospital in Boston. In the middle 1950's, there was a mock evacuation held there, and the purpose was to free the facilities of the General Hospital in order to accommodate a portion of the estimated 100,000 persons who would require immediate medical care if an "A-bomb attack" were made upon strategic Boston. Clark and Reid Company, Inc., Boston, was one of the companies requested to supply vans for the evacuation.

The practice run in those days was repeated often, and this

drill was most efficient in getting the necessary material and personnel out of the hospital without alarming the truly sick people who must be moved during an atomic attack. Donald Martin, of Clark and Reid, pointed out that moving vans provided the only practical means of getting large numbers of patients and equipment out of the area in time. It is a highly flexible means of transporting men and their possessions, and even simulated wartime operations showed how effective it could be.

In the days when *Life* magazine was selling thousands of shelter plans for elaborate air-raid additions to one's house, and in the days when people were genuinely afraid of alien attack from the air, many firms throughout the land, in strategic as well as in semirural areas, were called upon to make a contribution. One must recognize how valuable the free flow of men and materials would be to an evacuation of a given area. If one has ever been to Vietnam and seen what an air raid can do with conventional weapons to a main road, one can tell how necessary the moving van can be to simply *go* where nothing else can to move people and goods. It was in these days of the 1950's that many people realized this situation for the first time. For example, furniture pads could serve as mattresses and covers for those in distress. Other adaptations, simple or complex, were endless.

The list of possible applications of moving and storage operators' experience, either to a real war or only to training for war, conveyed a sense of the way people were thinking about the industry in those days. The Movers Conference of America, meeting in Chicago, was given a glimpse of the way that the military mind specifically viewed movers, what the "image" of the moving and storage industry was to the man who must move and move fast to save his own life and those of others.

Speaking before the annual convention in the mid-1950's, James K. Knudson, Defense Transport Administrator, offered a candid view from the Pentagon, not in militaristic terms, but with practical, positive advice that could help the mover do his job better, as far as the military were concerned, and in the process improve the country's defense posture.

"I once heard someone speak of the moving industry," Mr. Knudson began, "as the 'stepchild' of American transportation. We have the feeling that your industry cannot, indeed, be classed under the general heading of commercial transportation, as are the railroads, the trucks, the waterways.

"Your industry is unique," Knudson continued, "in that it is historically organized to render a personal short-haul or long-haul service to the families of America. And in that regard, you supply an indispensable aid in preserving the continuity of the American family."

This statement, made almost 20 years ago, seems as fresh today. Knudson had some other thoughts, too, somewhat philosophical in tone, before he got down to the hard facts of what the government expected and needed from the movers of America. "Here in our country, we love our homes more than almost anything else. . . . As we all know, homes are extremely personal things. So personal, in fact, that after we have lived in them a while they become woven into our very beings—a definite part of us. Moving a home from one location to another is often at best a dislocating and saddening experience. Anything, any service, that can ease that sense of dislocation and upset, can reduce the uncomfortable disorganization that attends the chore of moving; anything like this earns for itself a permanent place in the sunlight of American civilization."

However, Mr. Knudson quickly got down to the heart of his concern: "I think you gentlemen would like to have some suggestions that will assist you to do an even better job than the one you are now doing—aiding you in building and retaining public goodwill. There are some ways in which we at the Interstate Commerce Commission feel that this can be done. . . . Protection for the public is one of the primary objectives sought in federal regulations of the moving industry. . . . More than 99% of your present and prospective patrons are unaware of the complexities and intricacies of tariffs. Every man in the moving industry should consider it his moral, if not his legal, obligation to acquaint fully each prospective customer, *and in plain language,* with all the tariff requirements which bear upon the movement of the customer's household possessions. . . . It is contrary to the spirit of the statute, it is a reprehensible business practice for a tariff to be used by the skilled to trap the unwary."

Although his imagery makes one think of cat and mouse, Knudson put his finger squarely on the heart of the question: How does one improve the communications situation between mover and customer?

Knudson laid it on the line and his response was no-nonsense, straight-from-the-shoulder. "I won't settle for the status quo," he said, to end his talk. It was an effective performance.

Various trends were forming in the 1950's for those with enough vision to spot them. Some would be extremely profitable for those operators who could take advantage and move swiftly. The storage of business records, for example, was growing to be more and more of a problem for business establishments located in high-rent districts, as urban centralization grew to be ever more difficult. For example, a company with a building at 52d Street and Fifth Avenue in New York City would not and *could not* use an entire floor of its building to store cancelled checks, social security benefit records, or old insurance policies. The examples one could cite are many and varied, so that many aggressive storage companies, because of this desperate need for usable space, were in the right spot at the right time—and the profitability factor has been extremely important right up to the present time.

The National Storage Company of Pittsburgh, Pennsylvania, for instance, even went as far as to lease a former limestone mine 42 miles north of the city where the Westinghouse Electric Corporation saw fit to store 105,000 boxes of records at 205 feet below the surface of the ground. Four employees worked full-time at the site, caring for the records. In fact, these people never saw the light of day during their tenure there. It took about three months to get the mine heated properly and because heat loss is very low it probably took several more months to get everything comfortable. This limestone mine had been completely worked out in 1940, and it covered about 80 acres which were owned by the National Storage Company.

Because of the presence of some security documents, as well as the need to store records in a place that was not in an expensive real estate zone, there was a special situation that Westinghouse had to cope with right away. Taking record storage underground, one Westinghouse expert remarked, probably reduced operating expenses at least 34% annually. It was to reduce costs and to maintain safety from atomic attack (as noted, a problem in those days) that prompted this rather unique decision.

This particular record center normally contained 37,000 cartons of company records or an average of over 3,000 cartons a month. Each year about 32,000 cartons were destroyed, another valuable factor in having the facility outside of town and in an uncongested place. The ecological problems alone of disposing of all this paper would be awesome — even in a lonely mine shaft, let alone in the canyons of a modern, crowded American city.

This trend became a nationwide one. Many companies in Chicago, for instance, started to store hospital records along with their usual furniture storage. On the crowded near northside, for example, hospitals and business offices located there simply couldn't provide the needed space for records that they were bound under law to keep for a certain period of time. In all cities, the same situation suddenly held true, and many companies searched for convenient suburban sites — not always as remote or as unusual as "Underground Valuables" in Pittsburgh — in order to pursue new profit possibilities.

The use of suburban storage facilities continues to hold true today for City Transfer in San Francisco, for instance, and other industry leaders. Many companies saw additional avenues for revenue in the prosperous 1950's, including Weisberger,

Fischer, Chelsea and Morgan in New York, and firms in other parts of the country.

One example is the Neptune company of New Rochelle, New York. This firm has operated over the years as a prime example of a closely owned and traditionally family-dominated firm, with a great deal of vision added to the operation.

The days of Neptune's greatest growth with International Business Machines and other prominent international manufacturers of sensitive business equipment were made possible by some large sacrifices and a great deal of hard work carried on almost 70 years before.

In the early 1900's, Charles Kirschenbaum was a junk dealer in New Rochelle, New York, and although the family is not particularly fond of the nickname, they do not blush when giving out the information. In those early days Charles Kirschenbaum was known as "Cheap Charley." He went into the moving and storage business with his four sons because he had to make a living and fast. When he came over to this country from Austria, at the age of 13, Charles, the son of an Austrian farmer, could hardly speak any English, and he soon saw that life was not going to be easy without this language in the New World. He worked on the docks as a stevedore at the age of 13, and, because he was Jewish, all his relatives expected that he would go into the garment business, as all his friends and relatives in the New York Jewish community were doing.

Charley didn't think so. He ventured north into Westchester County, after working for a short time as a buttonhole maker — a job which he hated, reports his son, Henry. Charley really got his golden opportunity by winning $1,000 in a Louisiana lottery, and with this money he bought a horse and wagon and started to chart his future.

In those days, all of Westchester was green and considered extremely rural by New York city dwellers. Charley started to sell pots and pans. Shortly before the turn of the century, he used the rest of his $1,000 bonanza to get married. Before settling in New Rochelle, the new family tried their luck in

Mamaroneck, New York, but business was pretty bad there—
so bad in fact that Charley had decided to give all of it up and
head back for the city. On the way back, in their horse and
wagon, the Kirschenbaums got off the wagon in New Rochelle
and gave it one final try. The horse-trading experience that
Charley had picked up came in handy. Soon they set up the
first family home over the local stable. Charley quickly built
a van of his own and paid for it with "a whole apron full of
coins."

It wasn't long until the tiny company soon became a large
one. In 1920, Ben Kirschenbaum joined his father and his
brother. In fact, many people today think that Ben was the
"guiding genius" behind the fantastic growth of this company,
for its organization differs somewhat from others in the business
and bears careful study.

As was stated previously, a good bit of Neptune's success
has been due to the sensitivity with which management personnel have anticipated change and thus the "changed needs"
of the big corporations, first of all those with headquarters in
the New York area, those companies with large and active shipping needs for overseas markets.

As International Business Machines grew, so goes a common
saying in the moving business, so did Neptune. The company
was an Allied agent at first, but decided *not* to surrender their
rights when the Allied split occurred. The company decided
later to join United Van Lines, Inc., but eventually went on its
own completely. By acquiring warehouses in strategic areas,
it has successfully maintained its independence. The firm does
not have agents; however, it does own its own terminals and
sales offices. They are wholly integrated.

David Kirschenbaum has been very active and is very well
known in the industry, while Henry is a past president of
NFWA; Henry is an expert in the furniture end of the business.
The company's approximate $25 million in annual sales for
1970 is probably the largest of any privately owned firm in the
world in the moving and storage business. In fact, in a recent

interview, Mr. Kirschenbaum allowed as to how his company now does more business in one working day than his father's operation did in one year, in the early development of the firm.

In 1970, Neptune had 23 locations around the world and approximately 1,000 employees. In this country, Neptune has offices in every city where IBM and Remington Rand have a major facility. It was during the late 1950's that the traffic managers for these two giants were sold on the idea of moving equipment as uncrated tabulating equipment, and the theory paid off in hard results for both parties. Xerox Corporation, Minneapolis-Honeywell, and other leaders in their respective fields have also been carefully courted. As the general corporation itself became more mobile during these years, Neptune often led corporate thinking in methods of moving more efficiently. Neptune was, in fact, granted the first authority specifically tailored by the ICC for the movement of computers and tabulating equipment.

Neptune has also closely followed the growing containerization movement, in its groping path to standardization, with great interest. It has developed as well as perhaps any other company the amount of business that is possible, both domestically and overseas, in the interchange of standardized containers by sea, air, and land transport. Such developments as the Sea Van Pak, the Air Van Pak, the Inter-Modal Container—all have been studiously considered and constantly refined, as changes in the art took place.

Certain other forces at play in these years helped or were helped along by Neptune. The United Nations development and eventual settling on the ground that John D. Rockefeller, Jr., donated was a profitable occurrence for the company. The UN is now an exclusive moving client. There is much diplomatic business emanating from the consulates in the New York area, and a great deal of government business is prevalent on any Neptune moving calendar. The company has come a long way from its most humble beginnings. Also, since that time, many warehouses have been opening in various areas of the country that show a great deal of change. Mayflower and other leading companies have opened warehouses by freeways in many parts of the country. For example, at the corner of the LBJ Freeway and Denton Road in Dallas, a 50,000-square-footage warehouse was opened, which also offers immediate access to the Dallas Freeway System and is in an area of North Dallas that accounts for a great deal of the overall percentage of moving business in that metropolis.

Many social historians have called the 1950's in America a time of reappraisal, of settling down to a "quiet" life of normal, peaceful living. Those years have been labeled the time of the "Quiet Generation." Few people involved in working for their daily bread in the moving and storage industry would have agreed, however, about the peace and quiet.

In 1956, for example, quite an interesting situation was developing in New York City, and it centered once more around the large and active Morgan family. For some time, the Morgans had been aware that the well-known business family of Iselin was interested in selling the Manhattan Storage Company located on 52d Street. The property in those times was exceedingly valuable, as were their holdings at 80th Street and Third Avenue on New York's fashionable upper eastside. The family wanted to divest itself completely of these two very important locations and eventually sold their business interests in moving and storage to William Zeckendorf, the legendary financial wizard—he of the round desk, the round office, and the large vision of himself and the business world. Zeckendorf kept the building at 52d Street for a while, but sold the building at 80th Street to the Morgan interests. The building on 52d Street was so solidly built, incidentally, that a special wrecking crew from Cleveland, Ohio, was the only professional force in the country strong enough to knock it down. The building resembled a medieval fortress in every way—including the thickness of its walls and the safety that it afforded to anyone hiding behind these thick walls. It was the largest storage company in the city.

Subsequently, Zeckendorf sold the building on 52d Street for $15 million, after owning the structure for exactly 30 minutes. The Americana Hotel now stands on this valuable site.

The 80th Street location gave Morgan some needed expansion and is probably the world's richest building in terms of the value of the goods stored there. The enormous structure was built after the Iselins had moved out of their previous location at 42d Street and Lexington Avenue, where property values had soared to such an extent that they could not afford to use it simply for that purpose. As an interesting gauge of what happened to New York real estate prices and what inflation has done to the storage business, the lease that the family granted on the property on 42d Street carries a ground lease for 99 years from inception with a yield of $1,000 net income *per day.*

Morgan solidified its position in the world's most densely packed area—midtown Manhattan—when it, as the city's *oldest* moving firm, bought the biggest company, Manhattan Storage Company, to form Morgan-Manhattan. Morgan now operates the 80th Street building, along with its other holdings.

All roads do not lead to Manhattan Island, and many interesting trends were taking place at that particular time in the rest of the country—with some equally interesting personalities shaping the course of the industry's progress. In Cleveland, for example, in the late 1950's, A. A. Friedel was named President *and* Treasurer of the Board of Directors of The Lincoln Storage Company of that city. Al Friedel has gone on to become the President of NFWA and is truly one of the most affable and knowledgeable men in the business.

In Chicago, Martin Kennelly was perhaps the moving man most well known on a national basis because of his prominent position in one of the key cities in America. Although he did not have the long tenure of a Richard Daley, for example, Kennelly in his eight years as mayor put into practice the rigorous discipline he used so successfully as a businessman. He was fond of breakfast meetings, and his aides soon found that he called at all hours, early and late, because he was working at the same time and often had questions that needed immediate answers. In a tough town, he brought what one leading newspaper called "The Era of the Alarm Clock" back to Chicago.

Although Kennelly was the mayor of the nation's second largest city, others were making their marks too. As one issue of *The Furniture Warehouseman* pointed out, at one time or another, the moving and storage industry had mayors serving in cities like Fort Worth, Texas, Buffalo, New York, and Winston-Salem, North Carolina, in addition to Chicago. The contributions of these capable men made the entire nation run more smoothly.

In Chicago, there were other dedicated men, honored at the time for their contribution to keeping the nation's goods moving fast and well. In the late 1950's, hundreds of people gathered in the Palmer House in Chicago to honor Edward Byrnes, known then as the dean of the industry. He was present at the inception of NFWA. In his years as Executive Secretary of the Association, NFWA more than doubled its membership. He and Joseph Hollander, Secretary of NFWA and President of Hollander Storage and Moving Company, Inc., Chicago, Illinois, and others were as important as any men anywhere in molding the whole midcontinent force of NFWA, and thus the industry, as noted before in this history.

In the heart of the midcontinent, Chicago, many colorful personalities have been in action for a long time. One particular good source of information for this reporter was Mort Joyce, President of Joyce Brothers Storage and Van Company. When Mort's father, uncle, and aunt came over from County Galway in Ireland to the Chicago area, they probably didn't have any idea of how far-reaching their initial outings in the moving and storage business would take them.

Mort and his late brother, Richard E. Joyce, who died in November of 1961, expanded into Wisconsin and Michigan, as

well as forming two different branches in the Chicago area . . .
one for the northside and one for the south. After the two
brothers bought out the older generation, they expanded to buy
a storage warehouse in Wilmette, Illinois; warehouses in
Neenah, Wisconsin (to be near the flourishing paper business
in that part of the country); and in 1959 they expanded to
Detroit, Michigan, where business was booming and where
operations would be close enough to the Chicago base to keep
a close eye on things.

Also in Chicago, the Jackson Storage and Van Company, Inc.,
run colorfully and well for many years by Tom Jackson, is now
managed by Bill Conklin, Jr., who was no relation to Tom
Jackson. Jackson Storage, upon the death of Mr. Jackson,
turned its stock over to its employees. After starting with the
traditional horse-and-wagon operation, taking on all kinds of
hauling jobs, in the Chicago area, the company concentrated
much of its effort on the overwhelming move by householders
to the suburbs.

Bill Conklin has been an outstanding member of his industry,
serving on numerous committees and as head of the Chicago
Roundtable Club, and is known today as particularly able in the
field of insurance matters, as they affect the industry.

Also important in this most mobile town has been the firm of
Werner-Kennelly, which also left its stock to its employees after
the death of Martin Kennelly. In fact, its well-known address on
North Clark Street is now the site for the construction of a huge
high-rise apartment building—which says a great deal for the
eventual move of the moving and storage business with the
times. Often the industry has had to be in the forefront of society's changes, and the Chicago examples cited above truly
prove this to be true.

Some very interesting trends were beginning to form in those
"quiet" times of the late 1950's. Regarding the storage side of
the business, for example, one of the most telling reports indicated that toward the end of the decade storage was contribu-

ting 19.6% of the average firm's total revenue (of those responding to the survey), and there was a net profit before taxes of 12.6% of storage revenue. In the same report, 48% of the answering firms said that *all* their revenue came from *household goods*.

Perhaps, one of the most important factors in a number of surveys taken at the time, but particularly in this one, was the average respondent's general unfamiliarity with his own storage business — what percentage of total business it represented and what it actually cost him to run it. This is a trend that is still reflected in some of the cost-accounting difficulties moving and storage firms face today. In one case, for example, one firm said it had "100%" of its business in storage. When the firm was actually visited by a researcher, it was discovered "that only 30% of the warehouse space was filled with commercial storage and it had been this way for the past several years."

Donald R. Markham's annual summary of the current economic position of the moving and storage industry of 1958 contained some valuable information. The then Assistant Executive Director of NFWA put his statistical finger on some problems and on some growth features that were indicative of the late 1950's, pertinent for those times but crucial to present-day activities, too.

There was something disquieting about the figures that Don Markham cited for the year 1957, for example: volume increased while profits sagged, perhaps an indication of a soft economy or a sagging growth position caused by erratic political fortunes or general world conditions. The point seemed to be that the industry simply could not control nor isolate its real charges for labor. In a survey in which the average volume reported by the submitting companies was $401,400.00 (incidentally, showing a growth rate of almost 10% for the previous six years), it was found that almost two-thirds of the revenue in the business came from the trucking operation. A brief analysis ran as follows: 63.3% of total revenue came from the trucking operation; of this total, 32.1% came from long-distance moving, 25.2% from local moving, and 6.0% from commission income. Storage departments developed 22.1% of total revenue, and packing and crating developed 14.6% of the total revenue produced.

In three previous years there was a very close parallel between ratio of wages to revenue and ultimate net profit. If nothing else was to be gained from this exhaustive report, it became evident that the mover — big company or owner-operator — didn't control effectively enough his use of manpower and the costs of this manpower.

More to the point was the relationship drawn between trucking and storage and the ultimate contribution of the two functions to net profit. Of total net profit before taxes, 47.5% was produced by the storage operation and 44.3% by packing and crating, while commission income represented 8.2% of net profits. A simple statement could therefore be drawn: that portion of the business that produces the greatest part of the revenue does not effectively contribute to profits.

With this kind of picture in mind, one wonders if the prudent businessman wouldn't concentrate *completely* on storage; but, of course, he cannot.

There must be a way, said Markham, to make more out of the palletization and other trends of the times, of containerization and other standardizing methods. Many of the problems of cost control were now being effectively studied by the newly created Technical Foundation programs and the work of the Field Representatives of NFWA. Still, the course seemed so clear then, but the problems evidently so hard to solve.

However, not all was grim news at the end of the decade. The American International Exhibition in Moscow at the Moscow Fair, which had produced the famous "kitchen debate" between Nikita Khrushchev and Richard Nixon, also presented a North American Van Lines trailer that was judged "fantastic" by Russian viewers who watched it loaded into place to do its job. It was the industry's way of cultural exchange. Without someone transporting those kitchen appliances there in the first place, could the famous debate have occurred?

The van was described by a local Russian writer as "more commodious than most family homes in crowded Moscow."

Soon, the 1950's drew to a close and the oldest President to date, Dwight D. Eisenhower, gave way to the youngest, John F. Kennedy, and a great deal was happening in American life. Where there was change there was inevitably a moving van.

Still, those seemingly placid years were filled with excitement, right down to New Year's Eve, 1959. For the first time, a Soviet chief of state visited this country and had his troubles containing his awe at America's abundance. Although he might have been shocked by Hollywood's cancan girls, Mr. Khrushchev delivered without reticence a few opinions of his own that literally rocked the American people right down to their shoes. He rattled rockets, and in the early fall of the year sent aloft Lunik II and hit the moon with it. In October, he sent Lunik III to follow. This vehicle circled the moon and even radioed back photographs of the dark side of that body, an aspect that had fascinated man since the beginning of time. A new age, ushered in by the famous Sputnik of October, 1957, and followed by Mr. K's later exploits, was upon us. Man would definitely go to the moon now. Still someone had to move him and his equipment to his spaceship so that he could lift off the earth.

In summary, the 1950's saw certain clear trends forming that affected the moving and storage industry: a large standing military force would be demanding moving and storing services all over the world; the Federal Highway System would change the course of American transportation of both people and equipment as never before; the role of the corporation and its traffic manager who made decisions involving millions of dollars of business was growing ever larger; and the increasing importance of the profitability of storage facilities for records and other "non-household goods" items was inescapable.

Also, the NFWA established its Technical Foundation. One of the accomplishments of the Foundation was to provide a badly needed management tool for the moving and storage industry, and this program of improving management techniques has proven most effective. This need for management skills, especially in the area of communication and public relations, was to prove most necessary in the 1960's, the era of "consumerism."

6

The Changing of the Guard

If "quiet" dominated the 1950's, violent change and the emergence of completely new "life styles" dominated the 1960's. Suddenly, everyone was talking about the word "image" and what the image could do for you and against you.

One man to recognize this fact on a wide scale was John F. Kennedy, whose efficient campaign organization seized the opportunity to reach an entire nation through the power of the media. Although his margin of victory in the 1960 election was only 118,550 votes over Richard Nixon, Kennedy's victory was enough to bring in a new age for America. "It will be in the debates," Kennedy once told a reporter, "that is where I will beat Mr. Nixon."

As the politician creates an image, so does the moving man. He is seen in fleeting seconds of preoccupation and stress, but a memory of his performance lives after him for years. His performance almost always spelled the difference between repeat or no-repeat business—in the cold-blooded world of commerce as well as in the most sentimental of households. Some advertising on a national scale had been successful in raising the image of the industry, but much more had to be done in order to make performance match the promises of this advertising.

At long last, moving men were suddenly being honest with themselves. In the heat of competition and in the headlong thrust through the years to make often struggling businesses go, they had not sat back and considered what their identity was, what it could be, what they wanted it to be in this age of short takes and lasting impressions. Did they indeed have a problem? Many observers thought it was enormous.

Writing in 1961, Robert F. Odell, President of the Garden State Storage Co., Inc., of Freehold, New Jersey, predicted the situation that was going to develop later in the decade and described the course to take: be positive, don't forget your assets and what you do well, don't apologize for what problems you have which are innate to the business.

Taking his text as a minister might, Odell's thesis was that the "Moving Man Was the Most Honest Man in the World." Although he set up what might have been a wise plan to follow in the years ahead, the necessity of following these words was not yet upon the industry, and pressure was not yet severe enough.

"You carry an insurance policy on your household goods," Odell began, addressing a group of moving executives in the spring of 1961, "and personal effects against the risk of burglary. Everyone does. You lock your doors and windows, and have the police check your home when you are away. You do not trust the honesty of *anyone,* for experience has proven that it is not practical to do so. You always take every precaution to see that your worldly goods are safe, except for one time — when you move.

"Then you drop all your defenses and put yourself at the mercy of utter strangers, at the mercy of men who do hard physical labor . . . at the mercy, really, of The Most Honest Men in the World. They blandly go about their tasks with perfect self-confidence, sure of their ability to do anything that you require. It makes no difference what their race or education, or whether their skins are black or white, for they all have one thing in common: an innate sense of the sanctity of your possessions.

"When you move," Odell concluded, "at no other time in your life, do you trust so much in others; and you do so with perfect strangers. Strangers who are laboring men, but of a peculiar temperament. Men who have temptation thrown in their way all day, every day of the year, but who because of their honesty do not even consider that they are exposed to temptation. . . . In fact, a packing crew will go through a house like a swarm of hungry locusts. One man in the lady's boudoir, another in the crystal and silver cabinet, and a third down in the old man's cellar packing the power tools or even the empty beer bottles. . . . Then the heirloom paintings and the fine linens, the antique clock that belonged to Great Uncle Ebenezer, and the memorabilia of a lifetime—these things are turned over to the mover without question. . . . Grandma's rocking chair, the new bedroom suite, and the mops and the brooms from the kitchen closet. . . . everything is fair game."

Odell's speech was excellent and effectively presented. However, its admonitions were not always carefully followed. Still, there was a slightly growing awareness among various people.

This was also the time when a new term, "the generation gap," became part of the language.

"Somewhat belatedly," said one industry observer in 1961, "we in the moving and storage business have come to understand that the fundamental strength of our business is in the good reputation and financial stability of the individual, local mover. . . . Why is the reputation of the local mover at an all-time peak? But why is our industry suffering a black eye nationally? What can our national organizations learn from the successful efforts of local movers here in our state and across the country? . . . ."

This spokesman then went on to isolate the three basic problem areas, as he saw them: *rates, attitude toward new techniques, and relations with regulatory agencies. . . .*

In order to survive in the competitive New York area, for example, this man said, certain concessions to the realities of the business had to be made. "In order to properly service all segments of the public in our area, we have to recognize one basic point: that there is a place for large, medium-sized, and small movers in our business. The big company with its overhead is not economically geared primarily to service the small move and the smaller companies can't economically service the big move. It is quite simple: *you can't use an elephant gun to shoot a rabbit, and you won't bring down any elephants with a .22 rifle.*"

This kind of candor was not always practiced in every segment of the business, but many observers later have commented that it might have helped, in those important early 1960 days, when the advertising and public relations programs of many large and middle-sized firms were being formulated. In fact, the moving and storage industry has special problems that almost defy public relations handling—or solving.

For over 50 years the industry has faced the chronic problems of both school-motivated and lease-motivated changes in residence. Where there were no exceptional circumstances, the family planning a move would often wait until its children finished the school year, and this philosophy holds some truth, although there are differing viewpoints today about the absolute value of this practice.

However, the question of the staggering of lease renewals over an entire 12-month period has met a stony silence on the part of real estate boards in most parts of the United States.

Still, the school question is a vital one. Not only does it seem pertinent to the moving industry in its effect on present and future operations, as far as profitability and high use of available manpower is concerned, but also school plant use over a 12-month period offers a great social benefit, one that transcends merely economic considerations. For, if children are to use the expensive physical plants that have been recently built in this country, including swimming pools, wall-to-wall carpeting, extensive audio-visual equipment installation, etc., then they should have the opportunity to use these facilities on a year-round basis, say many experts.

Citizens from all walks of life are especially sensitive to this question, as anyone attending a recent bond proposal meeting in any part of America can testify. Here are two viewpoints about this important problem, one from a respected practitioner within the industry and one from the Chairman of the National School Calendar Study Committee.

Mr. Harmon Tanner, President of Tanner Moving and Storage in Detroit, Michigan, speaking in the early 1960's, presented some realistic figures to movers about their own enlightened self-interest in their community programs for the 12-month school plan:

"Under the proposed cyclical plan for a 12-month school year," said Mr. Tanner, speaking before the Michigan Warehousemen's Association, "a school with the capacity for 600 students, under the conventional nine-month school plan, would be able to serve 800 students. Under the cyclical system, this would represent a 33% increase in the use of present school facilities. . . . The effect on taxpayers is an obvious one: they can expect to save about 25% of previous monies for new construction made necessary in a nine-month school program. . . ." The point brought home to movers was that many problems for efficient management of resources could be eliminated if the individual citizen would push hard for this necessary reform.

"In all probability," Tanner went on, "the plan would have to be adopted at a state level. We should let the individuals upon whom rests the responsibility for education know our concern and interest in this problem. We should not allow this subject to become like the weather . . . something that everyone talks about but something that no one *does* anything about."

In almost ten years' time, the combined thrust of an industry that could benefit so directly from the 12-month school plan just simply has not been very effective in pursuing both individual and collective aims.

Speaking to this point later in the same year, George M. Jensen, as mentioned before, chairman of the National School Calendar Study Committee, expressed himself strongly in a speech to a group of moving men in Atlanta, Georgia:

"For purely selfish motives you and your industry should be active in bringing about year-round school. . . . These new proposals put education into the 20th century where it belongs, because the idea of closing the schools in the summer is a throw back to the time when we were a farm-oriented manual labor economy, and our kids and even the teachers were needed to plant, cultivate, harvest and process the produce of the fields. . . . Most plans invite and some require a complete or at least partial restructuring of the curriculum to make it more flexible, effective and relevant to the educational needs of today. This re-evaluation of the total school program will result in far more effective use of our already established capacity to teach.

"This is one of the most significant of the dividends to be expected from any well-thought out plan of year-round school. . . . Virtually all such plans make it possible but not mandatory for ambitious, highly motivated teachers—especially men—to be employed 12 months of the year at commensurately higher salaries then they now receive. . . . The absence of the father as head of the household from thousands of inner city and other underprivileged families has created a need, more crucial than ever, for more male teachers in our schools, especially at the elementary level. This need can be met only by offering male teachers full-time employment at full-time compensation as made possible by year-round school. . . ."

If Mr. Jensen seemed to be an idealistic social reformer, he quickly destroyed this illusion a few moments later. "The rotating or sequencing of vacation periods throughout the year which is accomplished by most all-year school proposals would have significant and salutary effects not only on the moving business but on many others—the travel, resort, motel and recreation industries. . . ."

It simply made good sense to use these expensive school

plants all year. It would prepare students for the real world
of business outside, where no one left for three months at a time
and expected to come back and pick up where he left off;
where the production of anything on a regular basis was crucial
for the successful completion of any task. Mr. Jensen obviously
hoped to motivate the moving audience, to action. . . . to doing
something.

Unfortunately, not much happened to make the most of this
sound advice. On another front, however, much was happening in American business life that would be relevant to the
moving and storage industry. The new movement was called
"consumerism" and its effects were too close to home to attempt
to avoid. This movement was not as removed or as academic
as the effective use of expensive physical plants around the
United States. "Consumerism" affected the relationship between supplier and customer and the effects took place, visibly,
every day of the working year, in almost every industry.

Perhaps one man has had more to do with bringing about
this new consumer awareness than any other in America. This
man definitely thinks that things have become too big in this
country. Huge corporations and huge government agencies
are simply unresponsive, due to their very structure, and unable to react to any individual's complaint or problem—no
matter how severe the hardship or how destructive the situation is to the private citizen.

This crusading man is Ralph Nader, and he needs no introduction to any reader familiar with the contemporary scene in
America. Recently, Nader consented to see a reporter in his
own home, a second-floor flat in a slightly rundown brownstone
building on Washington's northwest side. It was Saturday evening, and most people were attending some party or were simply
unwinding at home from a week of conferences and paper
work.

Ralph Nader was not relaxing. He was working over his own
papers, which were spread all over the apartment. He was reading and making notes and calling subordinates who are expect-

ed to keep as long hours as he does. He has a mission, this young man, and the mission is to show how people can do something to "fight City Hall."

Although his remarks were not altogether directly related here to moving and storage, Nader has commented on the industry in various speeches and books.

No one smokes around Ralph Nader, and this is one of the first concessions that any reporter has to make. Nader's award of a rather large sum of money in his successful suit against General Motors for snooping against him several years ago has evidently all gone into his various investigations.

His fashion habits have not changed since he received this money. His rumpled suit and frayed shirtsleeves went well with the rolled down blue socks that fell heavily over his scuffed brown shoes.

Nader thinks that it is high time to develop a dimension of the law where you have public interest lawyers who fight for what they think is right. In his opinion, there is a difference between an *attorney* and a *lawyer:* An attorney represents a particular client, while a lawyer represents the public interest as he sees it.

When asked why he felt such zeal about helping the private individual against big corporations or big government, he responded with perhaps the first and only personal comment made that evening: "I was fortunate to have the kind of parents who gave me a sense of conscience. I was hanging around courtrooms by the time I was four years of age. And I always had the concept that the conscience of a lawyer should represent people and not special economic interests."

In another context, he explored his own purpose in life and what made him the way he is, and why he has had such a profound effect on the consumers of America—and thus on all businessmen who service this consumer.

"I spent a lot of time, for example, in the Connecticut woods, where I had time to think and time to dream." Growing more enthusiastic as the evening wore on, Nader explained why he is so dedicated and why largely out of his own efforts the consumer movement has gained such momentum in the 1960's and 1970's. He had a word or two for every businessman who serves the public interest, including the moving and storage man.

"Corporations are far more at fault than anyone else," Nader said. "Among other things, they violate the water pollution law; this 1899 law has been violated widely, openly, and flagrantly for 72 years. . . . It's unpatriotic to tear down the American flag. Why isn't it unpatriotic to contaminate and despoil the land and water that make up America? I think what's important is to get America's ethics turned around properly."

This last statement, no matter how one feels about the intentions, wisdom, and rightness of the author, bears directly on the moving and storage industry's continuing relationship with these same American people who are reading, listening to, and being affected by Ralph Nader.

In the various recent statements, Nader and his staff aides have devoted some considerable space to the problems of the industry and how these problems could be solved. Again, without defense or apology, these statements must be considered in any comprehensive history of the business. Powerful men in corporations—and other crusaders like Ralph Nader—have contributed to the industry's identity as it has evolved to the present day. And most importantly, they will affect this identity in the future.

Warren Magnusson is one of the most powerful "in" senators at work today. Many observers think he is, perhaps, now the most adept legislator since the death of Richard Russell. In the tradition of Lyndon Johnson and other members of Congress, he knows where power and influence are. He has mounted a vigorous campaign of late for consumer interests and has received some interesting testimony and correspondence, both of which say a great deal about life in these United States, in this age of the consumer. Here is an excerpt:

"Dear Senator Magnusson:

"There is a ludicrously wide credibility gap between the charming advertising of the moving industry and their actual performance and ethics. . . . Moving is a difficult enough task without being cheated in the bargain! Whatever Congress can do to force movers to be good Americans will be appreciated by hundreds of thousands of citizens yearly! Yours sincerely, Mrs. T. E. R." This is not an unusual example of the reaction of the country today.

No matter what your point of view, much of the recent criticism of the moving and storage industry has been flippant and overly simplified. The problems are simply not that easily recognized or dealt with, as many mature industry people realize.

A recent publication authored by Nader and his aide, Robert Fellmeth, stated:

"It is questionable whether moving rates are based in any way on costs. In fact, it is difficult to ascertain how the movers arrive at their rates. In part, the movers' rates are straight mileage rates, applicable in any part of the country. Thus, a move between equi-distant points in the Rocky Mountains would cost the same as a move over flat, southern terrain, even though the labor and trucking costs might be vastly different in each case."

One irate customer is quoted: "We feel the laws are rigged in favor of the moving companies—bills must be paid on the spot. How much chance does a claim have then?"

Considering this area of claims, which causes so much trouble and takes so much time, Nader goes on: "It is true that the ICC does not plunge any deeper than necessary into a time- and manpower-consuming case by case approach, but the ICC would not have to be the arbitrator."

In effect, he suggests that a system like the one set up in the New York–New Jersey metropolitan area, could be made effective throughout the country, whereby complaints are referred to an Impartial Chairman's office, which receives complaints from customers, investigates the mover's records, holds a hearing, and renders a decision binding and confirmable in the New York State Supreme Court. Most complaints are settled in two weeks and the service is free to the public, states the Office of the Impartial Chairman. . . .

As perhaps Nader and others do not realize, the setting of tariff rates occurred when the industry was going through some of its worst economic troubles. Uniform tariff rates saved the industry from extinction and the ruthless competition of many small operators who were cutting every cost and, therefore, giving the business a very bad name . . . along with putting out of business many honest operators who could add to its over-all reputation and growth.

A perceptive comment about this whole controversy has been made by Harold Blaine, of Lyon Van Lines, and also at the time President of the American Movers Conference. He said: "It would be catastrophic to our industry if hearings are held by a Senate committee and the consumer complaints aired for the benefit of the communications media. It would take us years to recover from such a stigma. You all known well enough that good news rarely catches up with the bad. And such an event would be well-nigh a double calamity for all of us."

Mr. Blaine was referring to a previous statement of Senator Magnusson's that said a Senate committee would immediately begin the investigation into the allegedly unfair practices of the household moving industry. . . .

In this same speech, Blaine said: "We can say to Senator Magnusson that although the number of shipments has increased 38.5% in the last four years, the number of shipments with complaints decreased 1.5%."

Up to the time of this writing, no televised hearings are planned or have been held, on a nationwide basis, but there is always the chance that they will. The power of the media, unfortunately, to show often the bad, makes very little constructive help for the troubled consumer seem imminent. If this seems negative or apprehensive, the moving men have good reason and precedent to believe so, but many feel that it would be helpful if the honest sharing of gripes and opinions, on a positive basis, could be held throughout the country.

A sharing of information, a sharing of confidence really is essential to making the business run more smoothly and will, in the opinion of many secure and confident businessmen, make the customer more sensitive to the problems that the essentially honest and hardworking moving man has on *his* side of the "consumerism" fence.

Recently, the *New York Times* stated what a consumer can do to check on any mover listed in the yellow pages in New York City. He can also receive a booklet from the Office of the Impartial Chairman, entitled. "It's Your Move."

This booklet makes an important point about checking the listing of any individual operator. He must give his address as well as his phone number. For the customer's protection, he should pick a mover licensed by the Public Service Commission or the ICC. The mover, when making a move into an apartment dwelling in New York City, must employ union people—which is also a hedge against the employment of unskilled, perhaps incompetent, itinerant labor. In other words, there are ways not to be victimized and the *New York Times* has described them.

In fact, the *Times'* award-winning reporter, J. Anthony Lukas, recently took an uncomfortable but illuminating ride with a moving man along the East Coast and documented it, in diary form, so that both the pleasures and the pain were to be felt by the reader. This kind of objective, realistic reporting is all for the good.

One of the world's best-known demographers—a man who has been quoted earlier here—is Dr. Philip M. Hauser of the University of Chicago.

During recent interviews, Hauser made a basic, somewhat surprising point: The most advanced industrial nation, the United States, has been an urban nation for only fifty years; that is, the first year that more people lived in cities than on farms or in rural areas was 1920.

"In man's history, only a scant blink of an eyelash?" he was asked.

"That's absolutely correct," said Hauser. "We are completing the first half of a century in billions of years on this planet as a completely urban nation—at least here in the United States. And the trend to great decentralization and non-urban dwelling in any kind of organized way is pure poppycock. That is, those dreamers who see man becoming a 'Ferdinand the Bull' and sitting under the pretty flowers away from the filth of the cities —this is just not going to happen.

"By the year 2000, we will have about 300 million people in this country and they will just about all live in crowded urban areas, where higher standards of living and increased productivity will follow the basic laws of economics as we have seen them in this country and in the world since the days of Adam Smith.

"People simply live better and function better when they have these jobs and job skills in close proximity to each other. We *could* decentralize in the sense of putting population outside of metropolitan areas, and we could develop a great deal of a decreased density of population within metropolitan areas by some pretty advanced technology in transportation and manufacturing and the like, but this simply won't happen in our time.

"We are going to become even more centralized and together in cities and we, in our own ways, are going to have to cope with it. For all businesses, this is something that marketing, manufacturing, and service people of all types are going to have to adjust to. The storage and the transportation of household goods will be even more crucial to the efficient operation of our society than ever before. But wholesale movement to communes where people eat wheatgerm and farm their own gardens with herbs and live all kinds of basic, 'organic life styles,' not needing steel, cars, and household-goods vans is strictly beyond the imagination."

However, with less sentimental storing of goods, more moves of apartment dwellers with less furniture, *more* not less moves per capita a year, moving and storage needs are bound to increase.

The air of most meetings during the 1960's was filled with a discussion of the government, the effects of controls (highly developed or loose) on such an industry that affected the public interest so directly.

Here are two leading opinions advanced at a symposium held in 1962: The first, from Frank Burns, Jr., of the Blue Line Storage Company, Des Moines, Iowa, was for more controls by the government. "Regulations, when properly handled, can be a boon to most everyone," Burns said. "It certainly can raise the standards of operations; it can assure the public fair treatment by all; it can mean that our companies will have fair competition from like companies; it can mean, in many cases, a better operation for everyone. . . ."

The rumbling in any audience reacting to such a controversial statement (movers are usually anticontrol) was fully anticipated by such a statement, and Mr. Burns described succinctly what he felt to be the central problem: "I believe our government agencies have fallen down. This is where we get into trouble. If the agencies controlled and supervised on an equal basis, then we would not have the many problems of today."

Differing 180 degrees from Burns's statement was one from a man living in what many people feel to be the last stronghold of the really free Old West, Dallas, Texas. His name is C. E. Bradley, Jr., of Great South-West Warehouses: "My company is fortunate enough," he began, "to be located in a state that is remarkably free of any regulation on the local level. We are free to charge any rate we choose for local moving and permanent storage. We are not required to secure licenses or pay a special fee or tax in order to conduct local moving and storage business. . . . While it is granted that this situation can leave the door open to fly-by-night and cut-rate operators, it must be remembered that regulation can restrict growth and hinder service by reputable companies. Tight regulations tend to lead to mediocre service, with everyone trying to accomplish the required 'minimum.'"

There could be some humor shown from time to time, even about the government's role in the running of the individual van lines's business. To combat needless bureaucratic paper pushing, you must have humor to survive.

One example of the decade's version of government game-manship is this report, repeated here in its entirety, which shows how one man fielded a query about his handling of the government's request for information concerning taxation, record keeping, and general reporting.

The item comes from a 1961 story in *Transport Topics*: "We are too busy complying with requirements, securing and completing forms, meeting deadlines, and compiling information for monthly, quarterly and annual state fuel tax reports, Interstate Commerce Commission reports, mileage reports, wage and hour reports, social security reports, federal withholding reports, state withholding reports, Tennessee *ad valorem* tax reports, Georgia motor fuel and mileage reports, North Carolina highway mileage and use tax reports, Virginia mileage reports and fuel tax reports, as well as several other states which require certain reports, state permits, license plates, cab cards, identification numbers, telegraphic authority, lease arrangements, trip tickets, windshield stickers, letters of authority, port of entry mileage and tax calculations, fuel importers permits, public service commission plates and registrations, and other petty paper pieces, that could result in a fine or penalty ranging from a warning, or small fine, to $500 or more and the loss of interstate authority or suspension of the Interstate Commerce Commission certificates, to help you by furnishing the information you requested."

This 162-word statement coming from a Southern moving and storage man showed that he was busy, to say the least, and deeply involved with Uncle Sam, but he had not forgotten how to let off steam.

In fact, a brief listing of some of the laws affecting the industry at this time and how they apply to today's modern business in general is essential to an understanding of what pressures most moving and storage men were undergoing through the 1960's—right up to the present day.

As far back as 1939, the ICC was questioning the moving and storage industry about certain practices, and in the MC-19 series an almost complete legal history of this often complicated relationship can be traced.

Since the late 1930's at least nine times the ICC has deemed it necessary to reopen MC-19 and restrengthen the rules. As the 1960's opened, numerous hearings, countless discussions and committee meetings, various proposals and counter-proposals, litigation in federal courts and assorted actions were started in the attempt to rewrite MC-19. At various stages in its history, MC-19 has covered all the important areas of every mover's existence: Specific rules that were added in the 1960's were introduced in order to create an atmosphere of full disclosure between the mover and the householder throughout the entire course of the move.

In a report of March 5, 1970, for example, to turn ahead for a moment to the newest rules, the ICC emphasized the need for full disclosure by stating: "The average householder, shipping his most valuable possessions, is not experienced with transportation practices; he is not knowledgeable in protecting his rights; he is at a disadvantage with his dealing with the carrier, particularly if he is in transit during the move; and is, therefore, in need of all the protection this Commission can afford."

In general the new rules and modifications of existing rules include: 1. *Reasonable dispatch*—This phrase *means* that the shipper and the mover reach a mutual understanding and agree on dates or periods of time within which the transportation service is required to be performed. 2. *Notification of delay in pickup and delivery*—The new rules require that the shipper be notified that his goods will *not* be picked up on the date or within the period of time promised, the reason for the delay, and when the pickup or delivery *will* be made. 3. *Estimating*— The carrier is required to give an estimate if requested by the shipper, and the estimate is required to be made on a standard form so that the shipper can make an intelligent comparison in choosing the carrier to perform his moves. The shipper must also be informed not only of the amount of the estimated cost of the move (as above), but also of the *maximum* amount of money on a COD shipment that the customer must have in order to require the carrier to unload his shipment. For instance, a load estimated at $500 would require the shipper to have no more than $550 upon the delivery of his goods—the estimated cost plus 10%. The shipper must still pay for the total tariff charges, but he now may request at least 15 days credit for any amount by which the total tariff charges exceed the estimate by more than 10%. 4. *Orders for service*—This order for service contains information which will be incorporated into the contract of transportation—that is, the bill of lading. 5. *Bill of lading*— This document must show the agreed dates or periods of time required by the reasonable dispatch rule, the estimates of charges and specifications of maximum amount required for delivery as embodied in the rule on estimating, and the entry of the tare weight on the bill of lading, before that document is executed. 6. *Determination of weight*—All rules pertaining to weights, obtaining weight tickets, minimum weights, and constructive weights are now to be under one heading. From the manifest it will be apparent to the carrier management whether shipments are being transported in compliance with the requirements of the new regulation. 7. *Claims*—No language releasing the carrier from liability may be contained in the delivery receipt. Carriers must now notify the Commission periodically of the status of *all* pending loss and damage claims and the reason for delays in processing those claims. 8. *Early delivery*—The Commission adopted a regulation prohibiting the tender of a shipment for early delivery except as requested or agreed to by the shipper and enabling the carrier to place the shipment in storage for its own account and at its own expense in a warehouse near the destination point of the shipment until the agreed delivery time.

A helpful booklet was prepared by the ICC detailing these rules and it is mandatory that the carrier hand out these booklets to the customer, prior to the move being made.

An effort has been made in the above summary to present in reasonably clear language the terms of these documents. Still, it seems almost impossible for the intelligent layman to understand everything.

During the latter half of the decade, an important case was debated at length in the industry. It was called the Kingpak Case and involved an Interstate Commerce Commission investigation into the operations of exempt forwarders alleging that many agreements between the forwarders and the warehousemen who provided terminal services violated provisions of the Interstate Commerce Act. . . . The NFWA intervened to protect the interest of members. The NFWA made clear that it was neutral in respect to the controversy between the van lines and the exempt forwarders, and its sole interest was to preserve the right of the warehouseman to carry on those services he had traditionally performed. The case caused much discussion right up to the end of the 1960's and is an important historic development which eventually affected almost 600 warehousemen throughout the country.

One other big happening of the time, in addition to the above cases and regulations, was a 1966 article in the *Reader's Digest* which eventually reached some 26 million readers around the world. Written by William Surface, a well-known free lance author, with credits like the *New York Times* and the *Chicago Tribune* behind him, the article shocked the moving world because of what it said, and what it didn't say. Some people felt that it presented a highly inaccurate view of the entire industry. One commentator, Meyer Levinson, President, Victory Storage Company, Philadelphia, thought that the effects were completely positive. It made the industry get up and fight this image, and it made it realize that perhaps there was something to what Mr. Surface said, after all—even if it was proven later that the author went to the ICC and got the complaint file and considered this his final research on the subject.

As far as movers were concerned, Mr. Surface never interviewed any of them, did not go inside a truck or a warehouse, did not see an executive or a laborer of any firm in the country. Nevertheless, the article, appearing in such a well-known periodical, was reprinted and talked about for years to come.

Such occurrences might have produced the famous Atlas Van Lines conferences on "consumer" information which have been extremely successful in the last few years, attracting both traffic managers from major American companies and housewives who are delighted to be able to participate in a candid give-and-take discussion in Evansville, Indiana. There is no secrecy, and competitors as well as friends get a great deal off their minds during the several days of meetings. Sylvia Porter and other well-known financial writers have commented on the idea several times. It is hoped that other meetings like these across the country will bridge the gap between the shipper and the carrier.

Morton Bailey, publisher of *Better Homes and Gardens* magazine, in a thorough report prepared by the Meredith Publishing Company Research Department, stressed the positive side of the moving and storage business.

It is fitting to quote Bailey at the end of this volatile decade, where life changed so much and the moving business had so much to be both proud of and worried about.

Of course, Bailey said, there were headaches in any "problem" business like this—particularly scheduling and claims—but the industry should emphasize the *opportunities* not the problems.

"Moving is not a one-shot proposition," he said. "The family you move for the first time will move six times more in their lifetimes, and the easiest business is repeat business. When you move a customer, just make sure when the move is over that you leave a prospect and not a problem."

Often, it is the objective, intelligent observer who sees through the forest to the trees. Mr. Bailey was trying, of course, to sell advertising pages in *Better Homes and Gardens,* but in his zeal he set the tone for the year ahead: not defensive but opportunistic and positive; hopeful, not depressed about the huge market of at least 50 million people who would move in the year 1970, in some manner.

At the end of the decade, certain major events had taken place with enough force to form definite trends that should be acknowledged. First, the American corporation, so important to the 1950's, certainly did not stop its growth in the 1960's. With this increase in growth, there was a definite increase in the role of the corporation traffic manager on the running of the moving and storage business.

Many people expressed their views in those years, at a number of meetings. Here are some of the important statements that set the tone of the times and hopefully taught moving and storage men how they might better serve their corporate public and improve the professional practices of the industry.

"In selecting a carrier I first of all seek service," said Harry F. Washburn, of the Johns-Manville Company. "Therefore, I must decide on past performance, on demonstrated ability to perform. I like to use one or two agents only, and I do all my business through them for the lines they represent. I choose them for their ability to follow instructions, to communicate my requirements to origin and destination agents . . . and to keep me informed generally."

This need for communications ability runs throughout the various statements made by corporate representatives.

"When I get complaints back from my people," said L. Ben Roberts, Eastern Air Lines, Inc., "I photostat these and send them to the carrier. I think this is beneficial because it can be followed up."

This point shows once more the necessity to communicate, this time in writing, in making a moving case clear to all concerned, eliminating misunderstanding.

"In the international area," said E. A. Millner, of Ford Motor Company, "we are now in the position to base our carrier selection on the most important factor—service. In my opinion, for the international division of a van line to be able to provide a consistently good service from or to an overseas location an experienced and progressive management is needed. Besides a van line being strong in management here in the United States it must be equally strong in its overseas location. . . . I can see great strides in the use of a container, for example, that can be driven into a vessel at all major ports in the free world. More aircraft moves, more inexpensive than they are today, will also take place."

In an era so conscious of image and communications, it is not hard to see that the mover must be able to convey his value to the corporation. The 1960's were a proving ground for many companies that moved ahead and many that did not. All had to sell their services and above all their professionalism, both to corporate clients and to individual householders.

The 1960's, with the emphasis on consumer problems, the discussion of a possible 12-month school year, the growing role of the corporate traffic manager and his corporation, the higher number of overseas moves and the use of standardized containers, the definitely increasing rate of mobility in our society— all set the tone of the 10-year period which led into the 1970's and the challenges that these years would bring to the moving and storage industry.

7

A Reporter's Odyssey
into the Moving World

The moving and storage industry in these times probably presents as wide a variety of business conditions as any in the country. A reporter could go into the luxurious board rooms of the Security Storage Company in Washington, or the rather simple and almost monastic offices and warehouses in the South, or onto the tough docks of New York City.

The private homes of the men this writer visited were just as diverse. A Bach fugue piped into a garden in a suburb of New York, a view of the sun setting behind the Golden Gate Bridge in San Francisco — all were possible for a reporter to experience.

This reporter, in a special kind of odyssey, set out this past year to see almost all there was to see in the business — from coast to coast several times and from north to south, from the far South to the Northwest, where the air is relatively clean and the steelheads run in the streams, to the crowded and fascinating alleyways of lower Manhattan, where only a *slim* horse could have ever pulled a wagon even when there was no traffic congestion.

In approximately 18 months, this observer talked to all kinds of people—millionaire businessmen, black dock workers, men who inherited businesses from their fathers and are trying to make them better than they were when they received them. No other business is quite so indicative of what can happen in a democracy. All is possible to someone who will work hard!

In New York, for example, one veteran told of how he was asked to ship liquor during the days of Prohibition. All he was ordered to do was not to touch the bottles, and if he needed money, as he did often in his youth, he was given *cash*. He *must never touch the bottles.* "There must be an absolute count," said his superior, a conscientious man.

And there is Jack Woodside who is trying in the area around Atlanta to help Lake Lanier stay free of pollution, and by doing so has inspired hundreds of young boys of the area who are Boy Scouts. He has a mission and often has engaged in civic activities like this in the last thirty years in the Atlanta area.

Above all, these men whom the reporter interviewed were activists, men who often were given big jobs while they were still in their 30's and given not a great deal of formal training in running a business. They learned by trial and error, and they often had their failures. They valued their experience above all.

In Chicago, this reporter had lunch with William Miller shortly before his untimely death. His was a curious business start, and one that illustrates most effectively how this business has remained so personal, while serving such a large segment of an increasingly impersonalized society.

Bill Miller's father had been in the moving and storage business since 1910. In the era of Prohibition in Chicago, Bill had been working as a student in his father's operation on the northside, when one day he suddenly found himself staring down the business end of a gun. It seems that one of Mr. Miller's clients had been storing liquor in various disguised forms in the warehouse and federal agents had learned about it. This is truly a picturesque way to learn about your father's business, one that is hard to forget.

Bill's father married his first secretary and she and Mr. Miller started out to build a business together. They succeeded to such an extent that in 1970, for instance, $16,000 paid only a portion of what real estate taxes Bill Miller must pay on his one operation on the near northside of Chicago. In the early days, several thousand dollars handled *all* taxes of every kind.

Bill was only one of many who were in the thick of the action in these times. In fact, he often spoke about the ease with which people could enter the business. "Why, for $50.00, a guy could open a warehouse, no matter how large it is, just for the license fee. . . . And in Illinois, the industry of moving and storage is under the *Agriculture Department*," he said, with considerable irony. "For a mere $1,000 I could still start in the business in this town, and make something of myself," he stated.

Are standards too fluid, are people too apt to drift in and out of the business? The question came up often in this reporter's research.

"Not so," says Henry Kirschenbaum of Neptune. "Many people have left us in the last several years," he told this reporter recently, "only to come back, because they sincerely find this business more exciting than the one they might have left for, regardless of pay raises or higher prestige or a finer climate or what have you. These people we have here are dedicated, truly dedicated to the moving and storage business."

However, it is still a loose business; the very nature of it dictates that. Even though the problems of accounting and the difficulty of analyzing labor costs are major considerations, they have not hampered confidence or dedication to the moving and storage industry.

In Atlanta, this reporter visited for quite some time with young Jack Woodside, long-haired and wise, son of the owner of his family's business, who does not feel remorse about his role in life.

He enjoys his work and his father attested to the fact that

young Jack could handle the younger help and the labor that the firm employed much better in some ways than he could. He had bridged the "generation gap." Jack talked easily about his friends in Atlanta who had gone into the bond business and were making $35,000 a year . . . or so it was claimed. Jack Woodside was a happy young man who was doing what he felt he was good at, enjoying the challenges that his job brought.

If he did not have good motivation, it was obvious that no external pressure could force this army veteran to stay in his place. He was a positive force in a family that had long been in this business. He was able to stay in the family firm, and his father had the satisfaction of knowing what he could expect after he retired. There was a refreshing quality about young Jack, the way he talked, the rich old quality of private enterprise and belief in the family business as a way of life.

To take the pulse of the country's moving and storage industry, one has to cover the entire country, visiting every kind of mover—large, small, and medium-sized. Starting from a bustling Orange County, California, district office that in one day sees more action than some rural operations do in a year, to a coastal town like Bellingham, Washington, to the hustle and bustle of downtown Boston, where trucks still work their way painfully along the Freedom Trail in the heart of the city, this reporter studied the industry. Also contacted in this journey to find out how the moving and storage industry worked were: Jones Van and Storage Company, Stamford, Connecticut; A. North Star Van and Storage Company, Milwaukee, Wisconsin; and Whalen Moving and Storage Company, also in Milwaukee; and in the West—Arcata Freight and Express Company, Arcata, California; Jeff's and Jack's Transfer Company, Visalia, California. In the South, there were: Haynes Van and Storage Company, Pensacola, Florida; and J. J. Carter and Son Moving and Storage Company, Louisville, Kentucky. Many more companies entered into the research, but the above sampling will show the geographical representation—the East, the Midwest, the West, and the South—where so many moving and storage operations are located and where their stories are similar but also curiously unlike those of their counterparts in the rest of America. The moving and storage industry is truly one that reflects in almost all respects the greater mobility of this country.

Ever since the pioneers left New England, people have gone to the West to find their fortunes—often to return again to their former homes. To gauge the climate of the West specifically, this reporter spent a full week right in the middle of a Bekins' district office in Santa Ana, California, where anything and everything might be seen in one day . . . and often is.

In an operation that sees at least 75 to 100 calls a day to the inside salesman, anything, cultural and economic, is possible. In fact, Orange County has been described by one resident moving man as a place where "you'd have to be an idiot not to be able to make a living."

It is different—and very active. On the reporter's first day on the job, a young secretary called the inside telephone salesman for this large national firm after being referred to the company by a friend. She asked straight out of this total stranger whether she should go to New York, Chicago, or Washington, D. C., on her next job. His answer was that she might not like the climate wherever she went, and he didn't really have an answer for her. When he hung up the telephone, he asked a visitor, speaking seriously, if he had to take a course in human psychology to successfully carry out his assignment.

This question was not asked lightly. No matter now whimsical or humorous the situation may be, the inside telephone salesman must be a master at getting people to listen and to act on his advice. His next assignment may be to move this same party again, and he knows that he'd better be more right in his advice than wrong if he wants that business to come back.

Whether the customers are former Chief Justice Earl Warren or Mr. Richard M. Nixon (who moved in 1962 from the California area to New York to join a Wall Street law firm), anything can happen in California.

The average length of time of residence in Orange County is three years, surveys have shown, so the value of repeat business is critical, especially when compared with more stable areas like Des Moines, Iowa, for example, where a respected moving man like Frank Burns may send *three* families to either coast in a given year and one overseas. There *must* always be close attention to service and to the variety of the customer's needs.

During this reporter's stay in the Bekins' district office, a day was spent in white coveralls on a van, simply observing the action. The day was illuminating and indicative of what is happening in America, in the mobile society, and particularly in the special world of Orange County, California.

In such feverish action there is bound to be waste. Out of 300 to 400 requests for a van to come to a residence, there will be about 15 to 20 cancellations of these orders, often without prior notice being given to the mover. He is tempted to take some kind of action, but he realizes that in such an active moving society like this, the end result of any negative response could be often catastrophic, for still the word-of-mouth reference is his biggest asset. This particular day there were no cancellations and every move was a revelation of sorts.

All kinds of people made up this moving world. In the morning, a young couple, recently married, moved their goods from storage to their first apartment, one that was monastic in its simplicity. The young husband had been recently a driver for one of this van line's competitors and now he had taken a job in the Santa Ana, California, area as a surveyor. This couple's possessions included a bed, one table and chair, and in the hall closet was a pair of motorcycle boots. The total charges for the move, where nothing was damaged, were $40.50. The man of the house had the politeness to offer the crew a beer when it left, which was just as politely refused.

The next move, around noon, was quite a bit more complicated. Many economic and social changes had been taking place that year in the areas around Newport Beach, California.

There was always a good deal of action in that locale. A call from a very cultivated, middle-aged housewife had been received. The lady wanted to move her possessions out of a 15-room residence that fronted on a quiet lagoon, a neighborhood that also sheltered the actor John Wayne and many of his friends. In fact, Wayne's converted PT boat was moored not far from this lady's own custom cruiser tied up at the dock of the $250,000 house.

A grown man could get lost up to the knee in the living room's thick white carpet. Everywhere there were books and original works of art; hi-fi systems were in every room, and every appliance known to man was available for this housewife to use, so that she could continue to add to the quite handsome tan that she had taken on early in the season. The furniture would probably measure out to around 20,000 pounds or more, said one of the moving men.

The modern decor of this California house was striking, so striking and so avant-garde that one moving man mentioned to another that it was a shame that more modern architects couldn't serve a season or two as furniture movers. They would make the ceilings higher in their houses, the halls wider, and the doors more generous.

When the move was finished, this reporter asked the lady of the house as nonchalantly as he could: "Madam, what does your husband do for a living?"

"Oh," the bright and charming lady answered, "he's unemployed at the moment. . . . Do you know of anyone who wants to buy some stocks right now? He sells them, when he has a job. . . ."

Only in America in the 1970's and, perhaps, only in California, could such a condition exist. Still, the Harvard MBA and the Yale BA diplomas displayed proudly on the wall of the master's den promised better things to come. There was always tomorrow . . . there would be another job. . . .

"Oh, we're going into storage," the lady continued, "that's why we're taking these things *into* storage. We know it might eventually cost more, but we also know that Dan will get another job, just as good, if not better, as soon as the stock market recovers. So, we don't want to move everything into a rental and then have to move it out again . . .

"Wouldn't you men like a cocktail or something?" she asked, completely unconcerned about her future, it seemed.

When she was asked about her very handsome boat tied at the back door, she answered: "Oh, that's been sold too. We are going to travel light for a while."

Then she was gone into her charming house, where she could stay for several more hours until her Ivy-League husband returned from job hunting to take her to the new domicile. It was just the breaks, just the way one lived in California, by the water, in the 1970's.

"Wouldn't you fellows like a drink or something?" the lady asked once more, when everything had been finished. "It's been such a beastly hot day. . . ."

In the late afternoon, this reporter and his crew called on a Marine family attached to the El Toro Marine Base not far away. In the doorway of the comfortably furnished but simple block house were six blond children, all under seven years of age. The mother, a bronzed, blond woman of about 30, seemed as pleased as could be at the appearance of the truck.

"Oh, am I glad to see you!" she said. "We've moved thirteen times in the last nine years and I'm an old hand at it."

"Doesn't moving it all seem like such a chore?" this reporter asked.

"Oh, no, dear me," she answered, "I think that the children have benefited from moving. I know I have. We have had so many babies on the road that they all know how to take care of themselves. My husband—he's not here, and I suppose you've been wondering where he is—he's in Vietnam right now. The children and I are going back to Cherry Point, North Carolina, . . . to wait for . . . him."

From there—the assumption was left hanging in the air—one never knew. This loyal wife of the Marines seemed to thrive on such change and if her possessions showed a little fair wear and tear, as the military would say, it did not faze her.

As the big white moving van left the driveway and worked its way along the flat streets, through the miles and miles of identical houses in the El Toro complex, the men speculated about what effect on military moves would take place if the military did become a volunteer army, did settle into a Hessian group training and fighting only for pay, not patriotism. An army of professionals might not have all those blond-haired, tough little kids getting underfoot.

It seemed to the driver and his helpers that something would be lost too—the big, largely happy families, the flocks of dogs and cats that often got left behind in a move. This is a way of life, a mobile society that only America produces that is perhaps our best product for export overseas.

In the Orange County area, where Disneyland sits gigantic and unreal down the road from several well-known moving company warehouses and district offices, the lead time for announcing a move usually works out to be about a week in advance. Even with the comfort that such a period offers, things don't always go right. People change their minds. There are divorce proceedings and custody fights about children, as well as the furniture. Older people decide at the last minute not to exchange a large house owned for forty years for an apartment. (After all, where would they do their gardening?) . . . And so it goes.

The first of the month, and again around the fifteenth, finds things hectic, and if there were a way to space out the work, both the moving company and the customer would be better served by such action.

After this actual moving experience on the van, this reporter spent considerable time with a Bekins' residential salesman, after first spending several days on the phone with the inside telephone salesman in the Santa Ana district office. In this case, one of the senior inside telephone salesmen was able to show this reporter, at the same time he was instructing a new recruit, the intricacies of his job. The level of competence, diplomacy, and control was impressive.

"If someone cancels, we can't do anything about it. . . . We simply don't let it bother us," said this veteran of 12 years. "But we do give the decided impression and communicate such an impression that we would expect that the customer, upon re-examing his intentions after cancellation, would come back to us because of the time we have already spent with him. . . . You'd be surprised how often this works—and how many times the customer's friends will come to us after hearing something like: 'That guy was real nice. We decided to cancel the truck and he still kept his cool. . . .' or something like that."

In fact, the inside telephone salesman stated that almost 65% of his business comes from personal references, at least in southern California, where there is great mobility of people, and information in the yellow pages of the phone book changes almost daily. This man had been unusually long in his present post, not because he had been passed over for promotion, but because he was especially valuable in his inside position. This was demonstrated when he was showing the ropes to the new man sitting next to him—and this reporter who was allowed to listen on an extension.

By doing so, this reporter caught the nuances of the entire conversation.

In busy months, this man received about 60 calls a day, but in a recession summer he felt that his volume was noticeably reduced. The callers who did come through were remarkably agitated as anyone can be expected to be who is moving from familiar surroundings, and a greater volume of this kind of business might have taxed the patience of a less experienced telephone salesman.

The "outside" residential salesman next to be interviewed had been promoted to his job after eight years on the inside telephone. His grasp of the community aspects of his job was equally impressive. He had a working wife and no children, and most of his recreation was spent on the ski slopes with occasional trips to Las Vegas or Lake Tahoe.

However, his real aim in life seemed to be to make a contribution to the people he served—and he showed it in a number of ways. At this particular time, another ruling had been issued by the ICC, one that would further complicate the consumer's life. The salesman conducted weekly seminars for anyone who wished to learn about ways to save money through the new rulings. The educational program was purely institutional, and no commitment or obligation was necessary for the prospective shipper-customer to move with the sponsoring firm.

Even for this most mobile county, the attendance had been more than expected. The outside salesman had written the promotional material that ran in the local newspaper, and it was sprightly copy that made the reader want to come to the meetings, mostly because it made it so clear that he would save money if he did.

There is no question that this salesman was being carefully groomed for advancement within the company, because he was a fountain of information. He also had some new ideas about how the industry could solve its problems. Above all, this man was a supreme realist about his industry.

For example, he followed events carefully at the local Mission Viejo housing complex, where junior executives came and went like the changing of the guard at Buckingham Palace. Owned partially by the Philip Morris Company and the Irvine Company of California, the complex represented almost $3 billion in combined financial investment. Not every section of the country could boast of such resources, but this particular salesman was aware of the possibilities of exploiting such activity. Of course, his superiors expected him to make the most of this gold mine in his territory. Almost every 36 months each family in the salesman's area would move on to another spot, either higher or lower in economic terms. The important thing was that these people moved somewhere.

However, it takes some personal resilience to be a moving and storage salesman in this area. There are many disappointments. One time not long before, the salesman told this reporter, a state mental hospital with hundreds of beds and thousands of dollars of equipment to move had simply decided to cancel. The state budget was cut. Someone in Sacramento, perhaps even the Governor himself, changed his mind. The salesman shrugged. "With institutional moves there are changes, and you have to live with them," he said.

The sales-training area was where this particular professional thought his industry had fallen down most noticeably. "Often," he said, "men are sent into the field without much prior training, and it shows. They come off their own trucks, hard working, ambitious, and altogether honest, but estimating and selling are tough businesses, and they have to eat. Certain things are promised and not delivered. . . . Perhaps the man had his wife doing the bookkeeping and he was the rest of the entire company," said the salesman. "They had to have new business to eat. It's that simple."

There are more sales seminars all the time, especially in this leading West Coast operation, but more could be carried on. "Even the competition would benefit from such activity," he said.

The Orange County situation is marked by competition of the fiercest sort. Sites for district offices and warehouses are selected by marketing experts and researchers with years of experience; the instant recognition of a company symbol, the right placement in the yellow pages. Above all, the image that the salesman-estimator, inside and outside, leaves with the customer, is crucial, for one-time and repeat sales. This condition holds true both in the short haul (within 50 miles) and the more lucrative long haul to another town, state, or country.

Still, the final decision to choose a particular company over an Allied or a Mayflower (our salesman's major competition in this area) is often whimsical and downright emotional. The color of a man's eyes, the look of a modern, stylish moving van on the road as it streaks by, the latest ad running in *Time* magazine—all have their effects on the entire moving population. The reasons for making a final choice are as diverse as people themselves in the household-moving industry.

The Bekins' salesman who next escorted this reporter through the course of two work days could readily testify to this.

The Hunt-Wesson complex of executive offices in Southern California is an impressive establishment that looks like a fashionable country club, with its cultivated gardens, its modern decor, and expensive art work lining the walls.

The company chairman, up to that time, Norton Simon, had an eye for decor and had been known to use the aesthetic as well as the direct approach to get what he wanted. However, beyond the carpeted and tasteful reception rooms, there are the cold facts of business life. Especially in the traffic manager's office there were the doubly harsh facts that this had been a recession year and cost cutting was the order of the day.

Les Decker had a boyish crew cut that concealed his many years of experience with Hunt-Wesson. He knew everyone in the company; everyone knew him. He seemed as open in discussing his job with this reporter and the commercial salesman, an old friend, as he would have been in explaining something to Mr. Simon himself.

"We'll run about $400,000 to $500,000 a year in moving business for about five carriers in Orange County," Decker began. "We have our problems," he continued, "as everyone does. We have the unscrupulous person whom we move who will try to gouge, to pull a fast one. We find that about 85% of the time the issue can be resolved. We've had men moved out here by Norton with 35 thousand pounds of furniture, and nothing went wrong."

"We keep a record, frankly, on what makes a moving line worth our time and effort, a box score actually. It's kept on a one-to-five basis, and there's nothing secret about it.

"It goes like this: In the state of California, we value Bekins' services very highly; we use Allied a great deal anywhere in the

United States, but particularly in the east and midwest; we also do quite a bit of dealing with United in the midwest; in the south central and southwest, we rate Republic high on our list; in the southwest, we have good luck with Atlas. We consider that our position geographically is a little special, slightly unique compared to other companies, and we have special needs.

"So we use Global and National on a special basis, principally in the West, but not necessarily in the state of California alone, where we use Bekins a great deal."

Decker went on in his straightforward manner to set the record up for us, to show how Hunt-Wesson constructs its moving policies: "In 300 family moves a year, bringing in the $400,000 business I mentioned earlier, we have three basic categories among our executives. Number one: a man in the $15,000-a-year bracket in salary; this carries an open agreement on the use of most services and what we pay for, with the exception of the movement of an automobile. In category number two, we will pay maid service, for instance, and we go to rather big insurance policies with large premiums, as you might expect, for certain VIP's. In category number three, we normally allow up to 10,000 pounds for a shipment, plus all the services that I've just mentioned.

"We've had some minor scrapes and disagreements, but our recent surveys have shown that the average move comes in between eight to nine thousand pounds. One very important man in our organization recently moved and we had to pack and ship *36,000* pounds of furniture for him—including three grand pianos. . . . So, you see, we also make exceptions.

"The key is service in this business," Decker said, "but the minute I feel that old service go down, and I start getting flak, or our costs are over budget, I go to another mover.

"On a more positive level, we've been watching the trends of the industry closely, and the possible ways that we can save a dollar here and there. Take the Republic Plan, for example, where there is a reduction in rates in the off-season, if you move *out* of the peak season. Moving in the off-season with Republic, just to do a little simple figuring for a moment, would save us up to $40,000 a year, if we take a simple 10% reduction of what I said is our overall moving bill per year. But it isn't that simple, of course; when a man is asked to go, he goes as quickly as possible to make Hunt-Wesson function as well as it can. And we've had considerable national moves in recent years with our various mergers and the shifts that have gone on in this place.

"In regular times, we've been moving people from out here back to New York, to Dallas, to New Orleans—and this adds up to a lot of action. We figure that a man getting a promotion and a move is still going through enough trouble at the office and at home that he doesn't need any additional frustration with his family move. We handle that for him."

Time was getting short, so Decker was asked about the future.

"Well, that's a difficult question—there's containerization, of course, but we've been hearing a lot about that for 15 years and it still has a way to go. Moving by air is coming on. You get off the plane, get your bags, jump into a Hertz car, and go out to the home you've bought and your furniture is there, too, and you're settled inside of a working day. . . . I think that is a rare possibility, but it is coming. Moving costs by air are still prohibitive. But consider the alternative: we pay right now $27,000 a year in hotel, motel and other fees; $900 a move for nine days in a motel. . . . That's the average."

It was time to go. "I've got several vice-presidents going out this week and I want to keep them happy," Decker said.

As this reporter and the salesman left the handsome offices and walked across the green lawn toward the parking lot, the reporter remarked about the pure beauty of the place, the palm trees swaying and so on.

"Yes," smiled the salesman, "it's nice, and I want to keep coming here!"

This consideration of return business, in any part of the country, is critical to attracting and keeping the large traffic manager's good will. At the Minnesota Mining and Manufacturing Company, which pays out nearly one million dollars a year in moving the household goods of its executives transferred in company service, a Travel Planning Section has been organized to control all phases of the move.

"Since centralized control is used on all household-goods moves, we have selected several local agents in the Twin Cities area," said Robert A. Strom, "which handle approximately 95% of our moves. Our moving policy has been explained to them and they have been made aware of our moving needs."

Since the 3M Company is transferring so many people to all parts of the world, containerization has long been studied and practiced on a limited, experimental basis, in order to cut costs in every phase of the moving operation. In a specific move, from Brownwood, Texas, to St. Paul, Minnesota, a piggyback trailer was used in a carefully controlled experimental move. Photographs were taken of the household goods as they were being packed. When the shipment reached its destination by rail, the entire load of household goods was again photographed as it was being unloaded.

The damage was extremely minor, and the piggyback shipment costs were approximately $400 less than by normal household moving. "The challenge is here for all of us, designed in a new method of packing container," Strom said . . . "Containerization is the name of the game. The solution to reduced costs and improved profits is how you pack your goods."

The challenge to obtaining successfully such large repeat business is clearly laid down here for the industry by such executives as Robert Strom. One man within the moving and storage industry who has come as closely as anyone to mastering the difficult art of containerization is Martin L. Santini, Executive Vice President, the Seven Santini Brothers, Maspeth, New York.

For over 30 years, Martin Santini has been actively pursuing his role in his family and in his profession. He is a thoughtful, analytical observer of the moving and storage scene. This

reporter spent considerable time with Santini in several interviews, toured the containerization operation in Maspeth, and
saw the huge, custom-made crates being readied for shipment
to almost every major port in the Middle East, South America,
and Europe.

The role of international moving and storage had probably
not come at a better time for Martin, who began actively working in this special part of the business in 1942. The overseas
movement of goods presently represents approximately 40% of
the overall Santini business.

Especially in overseas activities, Santini has pointed out:
"We are not moving freight, we are moving the cherished possessions of a valued employee that will make his residence in
a foreign land his home. Let's not have the move become a
traumatic experience to add to his family's burdens."

The interdependence of industries in foreign countries has
never been more evident. No longer is American business as
safely atop the competitive pole as it once was. The Sheraton
Hotel chain, for example, Mr. Santini declared, is now buying
its furniture in Yugoslavia and having the Seven Santini
Brothers store it in their warehouses until various hotels and
motels around the country need the new units.

This increasing commerce with all countries in the world,
with some more than others, has put the Santini name before
countless customers. Their location on the Eastern seaboard has
caused the firm to be seen constantly by the communications
industry in New York and by other influential "name droppers."
When this reporter mentioned that he had seen the name on his
very first visit in New York and that even late-night "talk
shows" often mentioned the firm, Martin replied matter-of-
factly: "Yes, we think the name has a certain memorable quality to it."

Martin Santini has been sought out by many industry experts
for his special counsel. One West Coast moving and storage man
with over 40 years' experience has admitted that he has sought
advice in many a session with Santini.

In the field of practical predictions about the important development of containerization, no one is asked as often to speak about the subject—and its future use in the business—as is Martin Santini. "As the containerization system develops," he has said at recent professional meetings, "truck, rail, and steamship terminals will take on the aspect of container yards, with a considerable reduction in the amount of shed space or covered-warehouse space required to handle a given quantity of goods. . . . The major development that will be required to handle the increased tonnage volume will be in vastly increased yard area and the rearranging of existing yard area with heavy, mobile lift equipment in the 35- to 40-ton range, with an 18- to 20-foot lift to move, handle, and stack containers at least three high."

Not always has the Santini organization been as large or as well-known as it is currently, when it uses a carload of lumber a day at Maspeth in order to make its own crates, by its own carpenters, for overseas shipments of household goods.

The original Santinis might not have predicted that as many as 150 men would be working in that Maspeth yard, or that the firm would have been paying as much as $10,000 a year to a beginning college graduate in the sales department, one who has had no previous industry experience.

The company has come a long way since the 1890's when Pasquale Santini, the eldest son of Albina and Zachary Santini, of the province of Lucca in central Italy, became restless to join the people going from his native country to America. His father didn't want him to go, but his mother encouraged the whole idea.

In 1896, Pasquale came to the United States and obtained a job with a cousin in the moving business. A short time later he sent for his brother Pietro. With the two brothers working hard, it wasn't long until three other brothers joined them. In April, 1905, they started their own business and purchased two horse-drawn moving vans. The first office of the company was actually inside one of the vans at the corner of Trinity and

Westchester Avenues in the Bronx. The office consisted of leaving the tail gate of the wagon down, upon which the business of the day was conducted.

Despite the financial crisis of 1907, they sent for two more brothers in that year and set up a small office in a shanty on an empty lot in the Bronx. The Santini Brothers were quick to see the value of the motorized truck. In 1910, they bought one Alco truck. Today the Seven Santini Brothers fleet includes well over 150 deluxe van and tractor trailers.

In 1912, the Seven Santini Brothers opened their first storage warehouse in the Bronx. Today, they are moving materials and people for some of the country's most famous corporations. In fact, a listing of some of the Santini corporate accounts reads much like the *Fortune* magazine "Top 500" companies of the United States.

Their heavy machinery specialty handling, their art department expertise, their aluminum containers for shipment in the new "747" airplanes, their consulting work — all attest to their eminence in their field. Even the New York Port Authority made a film of the Santini containerization procedures for showing throughout the country.

The Santini operation now includes nine installations in the New York area, four in Florida, and one in Chicago. It is very strong in its overseas division, where its "Home-Pack" service provides complete door-to-door moving of household goods.

From its humble beginnings, the Santini operation now employs over 600 people. It is indeed one of the leaders in its field and a bright light for the future of the industry.

Not all the operations studied by this reporter were as well-known as the Santini Brothers. Many moving and storage companies interviewed in the course of an 18-month period were actually rather small, but they have formed in total a significant part of the moving and storage business.

A recent survey of the moving and storage industry has pointed out that over 5,000 firms constitute the industry, of which a majority are small, family-dominated firms. The "small" firm is very hard to define, in any terms, for one criterion may be the number of people employed and another may be the amount of money invested in capital plant and equipment while a final consideration may be volume of business activity in a calendar year.

In any rating system, however, the role of the small family firm in this business has been an enormously important one.

One of the most interesting people in the entire business interviewed by this reporter was Mrs. Kath M. Fetter, who for over 50 years has been a chief executive with Fetter Storage Warehouse Incorporated in Chicago.

"I got into the business to make a buck, at first," she said recently on a bright sunny day at her office on Chicago's northside, "but I really wanted to perform a public service, to make a contribution to the people of a community, to help them somehow."

Mrs. Fetter's bounce and drive are still most evident at the age of 76. She takes a personal interest in her employees and expects personal loyalty that is only possible in a small firm. When in 1920, Mrs. Fetter wanted to move some of her personal things and she couldn't find a mover who suited her, she started her own business.

"Even though I was a woman, I found there was opportunity knocking," she told this reporter, "and with the help of a little money I bought one used truck and went into partnership with my brother, Fred, who had just returned from Army duty in Europe. We soon persuaded my husband to quit his job to join us and this was our first team."

Today, Mrs. Fetter is a well-known force in the Midwest and in the country, because she has long contributed to panel discussions, was one of the first women in the business in a manager's position, and still travels from continent to continent as many people go to the corner grocery store. "If you don't stay up with your times," she said emphatically, "the times are going to leave you behind.

"For example, this business about the apartment replacing

the private home. I don't find that so bad in our business. Apartments often increase business because there are more households to move than previously, with private homes, and there are more opportunities. Of course, there are special problems to moving people in and out of crowded apartment areas, with narrow halls on upper floors—all kinds of challenges. But if we didn't meet those problems—if *you* don't meet your problems in your business—you don't stay in that business long."

Mrs. Fetter does not romanticize the past. She has commented that it now takes about $35,000 in some cases for a man and wife team to buy a tractor in which they live as a family away from home, handling moving assignments around the country.

"And it is harder than ever to make a profit," she said. The labor costs in her business now assume about 56% of her total business operating costs, much higher than when she started out. She can remember when her firm delivered newspapers to bring in extra revenue, and when observers of the business scoffed when she moved to the present location on Chicago's Northwest Highway back in 1922. Not much was going on in that area, so far from Chicago's Loop, but Mrs. Fetter saw that this is where the population would be moving—and she was right.

Still, there are many problems in the industry that haven't been solved: the low net-profit percentages when compared with other industries; the customers who still want to save money by skimping on packing costs, doing their own, and then complaining later when things are broken; the inability to find and keep good help, although this is less the problem with Mrs. Fetter's organization than with many others that she knows. (In fact, her long-time employees often bring in others by word-of-mouth because the climate of the establishment lends itself to stable, happy workers.)

Mrs. Fetter feels that regulatory agencies have helped stabilize the industry, forcing certain firms who think that cutting prices is the best way to attract new business to refrain from this kind of thing.

"On the other hand, government regulatory agencies do increase the costs of doing business, because of the numerous reports and involved procedures required in many instances," she said.

In many ways, Mrs. Fetter's interest in her business has kept her young in thought and action. She has been far ahead of Women's Liberation. In fact, she sees the moving and storage business as one of the prime industries where women can early get a chance to work in the front office where "the heart beat of the business is." Also, as Mrs. Fetter points out, "A woman can marry into top management, as many around the country have . . . and they can go on managing after becoming widows, as many women have done, also."

Mrs. Fetter now employs 15 people on a full-time basis and hires college students part-time during the summer rush. She has indeed inspired many people who have come into contact with her. When this reporter spent a recent Saturday morning with her, touring the warehouse and the other areas of her establishment, her men were involved in loading a computer that had just been sent in from Englewood, California, for the First National Bank of Chicago's huge new downtown building. She also does much work with air moving and will continue to keep in close touch with O'Hare International Airport, just as she keeps up with the present and the future . . . *and not much with the past.* She is too busy for that.

Forest D. King of Enid, Oklahoma, President of King Transfer and Storage of Enid, shows the same infectious enthusiasm that distinguished Mrs. Fetter. King has been in the moving and storage business since the early 1930's, when he joined his father along with four other children. All went into the family business and it has returned a good living for them. After World War II, when King really saw the business blossom out, the five King families were able to make a nice living from the proceeds of the firm and still show a handsome profit.

King finds that the amount of moving he does is about 70% interstate, but the local moving has increased, as labor has been paid better wages over the years. Now, a man will no longer move himself from one part of town to the other, but will hire a professional, for better service than he can give himself, because he doesn't want to take the time from his well-paying job in order to make a personal move, even for a day.

King, a friendly, outspoken Western-style man, feels that the general public is finally getting over the fear of storage. Although Oklahoma is losing population, King feels that disenchantment with urban pollution and pressing population problems will bring people of the next generation back to the rural and semirural areas.

He agrees with Mrs. Fetter that regulatory agencies have helped the business, reducing the chance for "dog-eat-dog," rate-cutting business. "The regulatory bodies have done for the business man what the unions have done for the laboring man," he told this reporter recently.

He has five full-time employees now, and like Mrs. Fetter and most everyone else in the industry, he hires students, firemen, teachers and policemen in the peak moving times. Unlike Mrs. Fetter, who has not seen either the lease or the school-induced move do much to change the seasonal quality of the industry over the years, King thinks people are finally beginning to see that it might be all right to move a child during the school year and not just in the summer.

Very much like Mrs. Fetter, Mr. King thinks his chief satisfaction in life is being able to help, to offer a service enthusiastically to people when they need it most.

Another mover who shares this enthusiasm is Mr. L. H. Haynes, who was quick to point out that he got into the industry by first selling excelsior to the moving men of his area. Not too many years after, he was on the other side of the counter solving problems for people, as the other moving people have done. Haynes does a great deal of military moving because of his location near the Pensacola, Florida Naval Base. He feels government regulations are especially taxing in time and effort, and he has even hired an extra person especially to work on government reports. He would like to see the minimum-age law made more flexible in his state, so that he could offer work to boys under 18 who could learn about the business and still perform the required tasks of moving and packing as well as older men can.

Mr. Haynes is especially happy that he has contributed as much as he has over the years to professional associations. He goes to every convention that he can, and he has gained a great deal from the seminars and the exchange of ideas that one engages in there. He does feel that there is limited opportunity for the college graduate in his kind of firm—he has 25 full-time workers and about 25 part-time most of the year. The college graduate must of necessity go to the national van line in order to hope for much personal advancement over the years.

However, as Haynes points out so correctly, in 10 years college men may be driving the trucks of the moving and storage business if present difficulties persist in matching job skills to the education of young men and women.

Other small movers, in all parts of the country, were most cooperative in sharing their experiences with this reporter. One in Enid, Oklahoma, Forest King, felt that women had not been given enough opportunity in both inside and outside sales work. He thinks that there is still a "communications gap" with a public that sees the mover at work only on a very infrequent basis over the period of an entire lifetime. This performs a disservice to the image of what the moving man is really trying to accomplish. Many movers, large and small, share this opinion.

In Chicago, Dick Westerberg has prospered so well that he now leaves the handling of his business for at least several months of the year to his son and his son-in-law, while Mr. Westerberg, Sr., goes to the gentle sun of Boca Raton, Florida. His firm, Nelson-Westerberg, started in Chicago in 1904 and in 1912 moved into its present location on North Clark Street. The firm also has a thriving operation in Elk Grove, Illinois, and plans for still another very modern warehouse in the same location will be finished shortly. Working 20-hour days in the 1930's, Dick Westerberg knows how the business has changed, but he has had the chance to enthusiastically hand the business over to his own flesh and blood.

This reporter found throughout his interviewing this quality of personal involvement and service, especially among the smaller, family-owned firms in every part of the country. It is a tradition that is dwindling, however, in this country. John Malley, owner of A. North Star Van and Storage Company, Milwaukee, Wisconsin, told this reporter that he had read a survey indicating that in 10 years the approximately 350 van lines of the United States will be merged by 1985 into 32, or a reduction of 90% of today's van lines.

This particular man traveled as a district supervisor for several years, learned what to do and what *not* to do within the industry, and then opened his own business. He is now in an enviable position within the industry in his part of the country.

The attitude of the small moving man is surprisingly consistent, in this reporter's opinion: he is fiercely enthusiastic about doing his job well. "Competition" was mentioned to Jack Woodside, for example, in Atlanta, as a major factor in his business life, and his answer does rather neatly summarize the basic point to be learned from interviewing movers all around the country—big, medium, and small.

"Why, my friend," the middle-aged man said to this reporter, "I am not in this business only to compete. I am also here to serve, to serve people who need me to help them, at a time when they need it most!"

8

The Future

A prominent historian has recently defined history as a series of related past occurrences. Without understanding history, another social observer has pointed out, we cannot understand the future because the pattern of human affairs cannot be predicted. However, speaking to this same point some time ago, Henry Ford I said: "All history is bunk!"

How can moving and storage men and women of the future consider the past record in a way that will mean the most to them in the years ahead? The future will be a time, we are told, when people will move constantly, in a much more mobile society than we have now, always in search of the perfect life style.

The panorama of human action of the future, of the 1970's in particular, and until the turn of this century in general, must be pictured in a series of vital, pertinent questions that affect and relate to the moving and storage industry's immediate aims. The desires are inextricably involved with *people* and how these people will live.

A child is born every nine seconds in the United States of

America. These people upon reaching adulthood will want jobs that offer them excitement, security . . . and most of all a feeling of worthwhile service to their fellow man.

If this wish for the future of America is idealistic, it is not too far removed from reality, in terms of what many sociologists think that young people now hope for. That is, the days of simply making a dollar are gone for many, many young people, though they are still attracted by higher-paying jobs with greater fringe benefits. If their occupations, which take such a major portion of their lifetimes, are not satisfying, they will not hesitate to try to change their life styles. They know that they have the ability to be mobile—much more than their parents have had. They will not fail to take advantage of this mobility.

How will this new thought affect the moving and storage industry? Philip Gore believes that by setting a high example of service and job satisfaction young men of ability will be drawn to the industry. "A final method of attracting new managers," he has said, "is to set high standards for ourselves in community service, so that applicants of caliber will be drawn to the industry and will give us a wide variety of people to choose from."

In the same context, Mr. Gore has stated: "In a small, close corporation, the customary line of managerial succession is from father to son, but this is not a surefire way of helping a business, or even a son, grow. We must have a transfusion of new blood. We can't rely solely on the reproductive processes of the family. Assuming this to be true, whom do we want to work with in our industry of the future—and where do we find these people?"

If this new idealism is viable in the world of the future (and it certainly looks as if it will be), then what can the moving and storage business hope to see . . . in use of talented people in the future, in realizing its own aims of upgrading professional standards and performance?

"First of all, the young moving and storage manager must be given proper freedom to make some of his first business decisions in his own way," says a Bekins Company personnel executive "I don't believe in training programs that deal in model and unreal situations," says this spokesman. "I say, jump into the swim and make your decisions as you think they should be made. That's how a man learns, by trial and error, by experience."

However, as this man pointed out during a recent discussion, "There has in the past often been a reluctance on the part of moving and storage men, many brought up in family businesses with a conservative frame of reference, a hesitation to allow the younger men to make decisions, to operate with the freedom that they desire."

Often, the result is that when a beginner is frustrated enough times, he may move on to another firm in the industry—or completely out of it. The hope expressed by many observers is that youth's fondness for unstructured lives, the dissatisfaction with anything big and impersonal will discourage a young manager from going into a very organized, bureaucratic way of business operations.

Does this prevailing manner of doing business then really make it feasible to predict that the small, family firm will attract young men and women?

As was discussed in previous interviews with both Mrs. Fetter and Mr. King, they predicted that their operation could not hold a truly ambitious young person who wanted to move to the heights of any organization, simply because the organization was not big enough to offer these rewards. Also, the young person must be willing to make many sacrifices, perhaps as many as his fathers and uncles did during the Depression.

After a life of relative affluence and full prosperity, will a young person be willing to make such a permanent contribution to service, to helping others when he is needed most? Many people think so, in both small and large companies and are finding ways to attract and get aggressive young men and women into managerial positions and have them actively participate in the company's growth and development. To make this more than just assumption, to bring it into the realm of reality, certain plans are being carried out now within the industry, in various parts of the country:

1. Profit-sharing plans are being introduced to help increase personal motivation at various levels of management.

2. New training programs are being set up, ones that use the newest management-training techniques.

3. Job stability is being stressed, in an industry that is indeed "depression proof" and apt to grow with the inevitable growth in the number of people in the economy, especially the number of active businessmen and business women moving now into their most productive years.

4. Active college recruitment, which is admittedly the part of the bigger, more progressive firms in all parts of the country, is being stepped up.

5. Participation in technical courses and special management or transportation seminars is being encouraged and the cost underwritten by the moving and storage industry.

What are some trends of the future that industry observers treat as most important, most likely to change their way of doing business if they are to adjust and survive in the future world?

1. *The introduction of new money into the industry is critical to a wider expansion of business activity than has existed in the past.* At this writing, several moves have been made to advance this trend: some have met with more success than others. The Armour Company's purchase of Werner-Kennelly Moving and Storage in Chicago is one example. New financing, new capital must be introduced into the business, even where profits have not been remarkably large, if the necessary growth of service functions and the physical plant is to keep up with the growth in number of consumers. The projected growth pattern in the mobility of the American society has made the moving and storage industry an attractive target for large corporations and conglomerates such as Pepsico, Novo, and Transamerica Corporation seeking to diversify their interests.

2. *A new, improved program of both industrywide and individual, firm-sponsored public relations must be aggressively
followed.* The Atlas Van Line programs in consumer panel
meetings have proved most successful in simply airing the
gripes, the deep feelings, the predictions of the future of the
business on the part of both practitioners and customers, within
and without the industry. . . . United Van Lines' "Bette Malone
Consumer Consulting Service" which advises the customer on
the economic, educational, and social environment in the new
community to which they will move. . . . The Bekins' consumer
meetings are another example. Many of these have been held
on the West Coast to introduce the customer in an educational,
almost institutional, manner to the latest Interstate Commerce
Commission rulings, the ways the customer can save money on
his next move, the soft-sell kind of appeal that doesn't force the
business or the individual firm on the consumer, but states that
it is there when the customer needs this particular service.

3. *An anticipation on the part of the moving and storage
industry as to its future role with federal, state, and local
government must be firmed up.* Perhaps a nationwide version
of the New York–New Jersey Impartial Chairman's Office is
necessary, in order to anticipate and therefore possibly reduce
the misunderstandings between customer and mover, as they
have existed in such a mobile, dynamic industry. In further
regulating their activities, will the moving and storage industry
be anticipating and thus possibly reducing the effects of additional government regulation in a future world where big
government on a worldwide scale seems inevitable?

4. *A new, improved, and imaginative program for future
methods of transportation; city organization and transportation in and around cities of the future are vital to an industry
like moving and storage.*

The use of piggyback operations on a wide scale, the increasing use of a *reasonably priced air-moving service,* the use of
computers, tape recorders for cataloging and filing descriptions
of furniture and other items, the new techniques in warehous-

ing, new materials for packing, the new training of packers and packers' helpers—all are techniques of the future that must be developed and refined.

What will the new city be like? What will the new mover have to be able to do? How can city planning eliminate the terribly crowded cities like New York and Chicago, where traffic is snarled on moving day when narrow streets are filled with large moving vans? What good architect of the future will realize that a house, and especially an apartment must be designed with ample stairways and elevator service, with generous doors and room entries that make it possible to move comfortably at all times?

Dr. William L. Garrison, urban studies expert, has stated that: "The urban problem is a 'too' problem—cities are too unsafe, streets are too congested, urban areas are too smoggy. Actually, society has made great strides, but we have an expectation gap. It is the things that we are *not* doing that is causing the stress and this will not go away."

Garrison has urged warehousemen to look for ways of structuring society's needs into demand, so that industry can meet them and benefit. "We should worry less about the 'hardware' side (operations) and pay more attention to 'software' (the living environment)," he has said.

James Hudson, author, manager of Systems Building Planning for the Square D Company, and professor of Communications and Systems Building at the University of Kentucky, has indicated in a recent issue of *National Wildlife* magazine that a number of Brave New World possibilities could be more than possibilities—and quite soon. Exactly what will the New City of the Future mean to the moving and storage industry?

First, one key plan is a proposal to cover existing streets with a roof about 30 feet above the city streets. Secondly, with filters and a system of mechanically manufactured oxygen, our present city streets can become a closed system of vehicular tunnels. These closed streets would provide space for fast, efficient monorail transportation suspended under the pedestrian level. Also, car and truck traffic would have a far easier flow than before. No longer would pedestrians compete with traffic. Sidewalk and islands now set aside for "people space" could be converted into additional vehicular space for automobile, truck delivery, and transport. Last of all, ground floors of buildings could become effective delivery areas, and the confusion of double-parked trucks would likely disappear, making moving and storage-truck transport much more workable in city traffic than it now is. Delivery areas especially would be more functional and accessible to the moving truck than is now the case. This situation would also include vast new uses of freight elevators in crowded urban areas, making the delivery of heavy furniture on fast, efficient elevators a commonplace, rather than the rare occurrence that it is now.

Previous big storms that have handicapped cities like New York and Washington would largely be a thing of the past, and the digging up of streets of these same cities would not now be necessary, for telephone and utility power cables would be accessible in overhead troughs. Any airplane passenger upon flying over this kind of model city could see at a glance how beautiful, well-planned, and effective traffic flow could be.

Plans are already underway to make these dreams come true in the following ways:

1. The Systems Plan has been tried at the Cuyahoga Community College in Cleveland, Ohio, and at Edmunds Community College, Lynwood, Washington, and at the Health and Welfare Complex, Nassau County, Long Island, New York.

2. The American International Development Corporation is using some facets of the new concept in the design of its 30-story building in Columbus, Ohio.

The moving and storage industry could well join in participating at the outset with communities by planning for the construction and growth of such obviously beneficial programs. The values in public relations alone, so often hard to pin down, should be very real. For example, the younger generation has already demonstrated to its elders that it definitely favors going into a business organization that will not despoil the ecological quality of the society. By stressing how the moving and storage industry's activities are allied with these aims, the industry should stand high in appeal to the younger manager. The idealistic, talented young man or woman of the future will want to be with a *positive* force in the society, one that offers service. There is a rapidly growing awareness on the part of the moving and storage industry of the need for enlightened, imaginative, and aggressive young people to help solve these problems and accomplish these objectives.

A great deal can be learned about handling future managerial talent by going outside the moving and storage industry. Consider the experience of the Jewel Company, which uses a sponsorship program, a "kind of institutionalized paternalism." This is an informal "foster father" program for all young managers. It works this way: a sponsor exposes his charges to activities outside their immediate responsibilities, and to concepts and tricks of the trade that they will need to learn. The sponsor also acts as a sympathetic sounding board about various problems, personal as well as professional. Interest on the sponsor's part is stimulated by one unwritten rule: you don't move into a more responsible management position unless someone is present to take your place.

A Jewel spokesman described the program as follows: "Basically, it is saying to a young man, 'Here is your next job,' and gambling that he will come through. We must trust him, let him go to his job and not second guess him."

Perhaps this kind of training program on a wide scale could help the moving and storage business develop those talented people rapidly who might otherwise leave when not enough care or responsibility are given to them, a condition which of course exists in every business today.

In the small family-dominated company, on the other hand, the family must be able to provide continual management potential. It must sometimes look towards the outside. One of the most striking problems is, says John Friel of NFWA, "Locating capable people with managerial potential and attracting them into the ranks . . . training managers and preparing them to adapt to the business and motivating these men to put out optimum effort on a sustained basis. . . . Competent people do not usually choose to remain static. Every manager wants the opportunity to grow and to gain status and authority in a satisfactory job climate."

Often, this situation cannot be provided by the smaller company, and people move on to greater challenges of a more sophisticated kind in larger moving and storage firms, or outside the industry.

One of the most outstanding management tools developed recently for the use of the manager in the moving and storage business is the *Accounting Procedures Manual.* Speaking about this manual, Robert Cavanaugh, President, Monumental Security Storage Company, Baltimore, Maryland, has said: "I like to think of the manual as a road map to profit. In the final analysis, all the long hours and effort that went into the preparation of this manual were aimed at one final target—to help us all record the accounting facts of our businesses in a manner that will indicate currently where we stand and what changes must be made in daily operations to assure a year-end profit."

The gradual upgrading of the professional manager in the business has made h's behavior dynamic and lasting. Instilling in his men a need to *counsel* as well as *sell* is becoming more than a passing practice. In fact, as many more Master of Business Administration graduates and other professionals enter the moving and storage field, more sophisticated sales and management techniques will be used. A recent survey showed that 20% to 30% of business school graduates do wind up with small and medium-sized firms, not because they do not have the ability to stick with the blue-chip corporation, but because they see definite advantages to operating in a free climate where performance is instantly visible. This trend should provide much needed potential for the moving and storage firm, if it can match its needs with available manpower—and, of course, keep this management power around for a period of years.

In order to maintain this flow of management talent, moving men are working through such acknowledged experts as Dr. Karl Ziesler at Northwestern University and Dr. Dominic G. Parisi at De Paul University. However, there are problems in the academic-training area. For example, as Dr. William H. Dodge, head of the Department for Public Utilities and Transportation of the University of Wisconsin at Madison says, there is only one active school of transportation now, at the University of Tennessee. Still, there are technical institutes springing up all over the country for the purpose of upgrading high school educations and for providing special courses to working men and women in the moving and storage business who have not had the benefits of a college education. The technical institutes springing up in the major cities throughout the country also serve to provide college graduates with the specialized transportation background required in the moving and storage industry.

No matter where these people come from they will be better educated, and educated people will move more often. This situation, coupled with more compulsory early retirement in large corporations, will bring about an increase in the general mobility of the population.

The new manager will then have to deal with an increasingly sophisticated and knowledgeable staff and clientele, and he will have to manage a variety of technical inventions that could boggle the mind.

For example, in the not too distant future, a 5-ton truck with an articulated boom could drive into a vacant site, suddenly spew forth a plastic foam that would create in one day's time a completely new warehouse ready for occupancy. Foam-in-place construction would have all the permanence of conventional warehouses and would offer two very appealing aspects that didn't exist before: it could be erected in a matter of hours and it could be constructed for a very low cost. The new construction technique uses a new epoxy resin which can be foamed in place from a mobile, truck-mounted erector system. The effects and results remain to be seen, but the concept is truly revolutionary.

Other examples: A future dispatcher could instruct a driver to deliver a load of household goods to Puerto Rico, for example, over the sea, on a "cushion of air" that allows no bumps, grinds, or lurching problems.

A fleet of nuclear trucks of the future could be refueled only once in every two or three years. . . . A coded tape could be placed in the computer in the cab of a tractor, then a button pushed and the van sent on its electronic way—from New York to California, for example. Along with these developments are pieces of furniture that can be broken down into their component parts, the parts placed on a conveyor belt, and the entire shipment sent out the shipper's front door without a hand being set to it.

These kinds of operations do sound truly fantastic, but, for instance, in the area of computer operations, the fantasy of yesterday has quickly become the reality of today. For example, as Richard A. Hollander, Treasurer of Hollander Storage and Moving Company, Elk Grove Village, Illinois, says:

"Use of the Data Processing System has given my company the following benefits: Substantial reduction of time spent in securing van line revenue figures; handling of accounting procedures by less experienced employees. Since no figuring of percentages is needed, the computer is almost free of error. At all times, the company has a detailed report on what monies the van line owes the company or vice versa. . . . This report is in alpha-numerical order for checking and allows in a very short time to resolve all the large errors that might appear between the company's van-line statement and the one presented by the van line. In addition, the drivers' reports, the salesmens' reports, and the drivers' trip analysis—all are much improved over the difficult to compile types previously handled."

In summary, computer performance is usually superior to

previous operations. Of course, many sophisticated examples of computer operation can be seen in the industry today, and at this writing new developments are making the discoveries of yesterday passé. The trend though is to watch closely the value of these complicated machines and to measure carefully their value in figuring final profit returns.

Industry experts have remarked that computers work very well for some firms, but are very hard to put to work for others. Newest computer discoveries are not always applicable to the moving and storage industry because of its very special nature.

No mention of the future of the moving and storage business would be complete without a reference to the increase in air moving of household goods, office equipment, and other materials. First of all, as many industry spokesmen have pointed out, there will be a tremendous increase in total airlift capability in the future. The "747" for example has had a dramatic impact on cubic footage in the air. However, this condition has not yet meant a great deal to household goods moving, for the "747" has a shallow cargo hold of approximately 6 feet.

The future movement by *container* in the air is very much in the thoughts of industry leaders. Of course, household goods take up a lot of room, but are low in weight compared with many other kinds of goods. Airlines have tried traditionally to move into shipment that has greater density freight-weight. Since household goods tend to run to about 50% of the standard airline "mix" for weight of goods shipped, the airlines would seem to be moving away from this area, at least in the near future. However, with the new huge planes, there will be so much capacity that the airlines could welcome household-goods shipments in the late 1970's, according to several observers of the industry.

For shorter hauls than might be feasible in the "747," there will be heliocopter moving. Some heliocopters can pick up a 15-ton load and carry it up to 500 miles at a speed of more than 120 miles per hour. By 1980, say some industry leaders, the giant heliocopters of that time will be able to carry loads of 40 tons . . . and will hover over our cities of the future, waiting to put down their household goods on the back lawns of their particular customers. What will these households where the heliocopters will deliver their goods be like? How many people will be on the planet earth? By 1985, for example, there will be approximately 275,000,000 people in this country, with about 77,000,000 households, all demanding the newest in household goods moving techniques and management. (Of course, as this figure is being stated, it might well be moved upward, as demographers are made aware of new trends, new shifts in the population picture of the future.)

In addition, the industry has conducted many recent surveys on the effect of this society of the future on the American family.

The effects of moving on children have been widely reported in the past few years, at some times more accurately than at others. In February of 1969, Allied Van Lines Incorporated sponsored, in cooperation with Loyola University, Chicago, Illinois, a two-day symposium on the effect of a change in environment on the child in our society. Ten speakers, including nationally known educators, psychologists, and child-guidance authorities, presented papers on various aspects of the effects of moving children. Contrary to previous feeling, many studies like this have shown that moving *during* the school year will give the child an excellent chance to "reenter" his new environment, rather than having him sit at home for three months in the summer.

Dr. Austin Des Lauriers, a University of Missouri psychology professor, has commented:

"When there is change and variety, there is room for curiosity, excitement, and surprise . . . and with these things there is possibility of learning, growth, and personality development."

When considering the family, one must view a child's future role as inextricable from that of his mother. In surveys recently taken, almost all firms confirm the regard that they have for the female touch in moving and storage matters. Women are especially able to handle other women customers. Careful negotiations with people are often delicate, as fine as the finest china. Women understand these various sensitivities and are thus most valuable in the area of human relations.

The future structure of society will only reflect the structure of the other institutions making up that society. In business organization, the trend to merger and conglomerate is inevitable for the moving and storage business, predict many qualified observers. One influential, experienced man has described the following scenario of what might happen in the future:

A wide takeover of national household goods carriers by conglomerates, with van lines backed by large capitalization provided by the holding company buying or building their own warehouses, instead of operating through the present type of agency structure.

These same van lines will probably buy out existing companies to gain needed management personnel, and gain an immediate identity in the individual community, and start with a going business rather than starting from scratch. This kind of van line will probably build only in areas where no existing warehouse is available.

To keep pace, other van lines will go public, where they were previously privately held or owned by agents. These public companies will follow the same pattern of buying and owning their own agents.

Many independent carriers will merge into national carriers, and others may be granted national authority, following the same pattern as above.

Where ownership of agents by carriers is impractical, the structure will move toward a franchised rather than an agency setup, so that the carrier can exercise a direct control on local operations.

Just to continue what might well be a chain effect, several larger warehouses will sell to conglomerates which will serve either as the conglomerate's entry into the household goods field, or it may be that the moving service is related in some way to the activities of the parent company which otherwise fit the long-range acquisition program of the conglomerate. Some few warehouses, however, may go public and take over small or medium-sized van lines in a "reverse process" of the above.

Indeed, family membership of medium and large warehouse operations will be greatly reduced and professional managers rapidly introduced. However, small local operators and small carriers with limited authority will continue to remain family-owned and continue to thrive—on a lower rate structure.

No matter what, competition will become keen, with less tolerance for lower rates on the part of intermediate and small-sized carriers by large carriers which are public companies or conglomerate-owned . . . and which will own a large number of their warehouses.

Other developments will undoubtedly take place, outside of these predictions. For example, some forwarders may go public and purchase warehouse operations in order to stay competitive with van lines, but cannot, legally, take direct control of van lines.

One element in the above description is most important to a consideration of the future: the "drastic reduction of family ownership of moving and storage firms." One man who has had a great deal to say about this situation and has commented with great authority also, because of his position in the industry, is Ralph C. Rolapp, Secretary-Treasurer, Beverly Hills Transfer and Storage Company, Beverly Hills, California, and past Chairman of the Board of Allied Van Lines, Incorporated.

"If our agents just become another cog in a large wheel, then Allied will lose one of its strongest advantages," he has pointed out.

In a thoughtful comment made very recently to this reporter, Mr. Rolapp said: "I feel the most pressing problem that faces the industry is that of extreme regulations and the high cost of doing business. I believe that college students can be attracted because of the great need of creative minds to develop new ways and means of transporting household goods through other methods that will enable cost reductions to take place. I have in mind containerization, consolidation, shuttle-service, etc. . . . I'm sure the reason the college student has not been attracted is because he is not familiar with the industry. . . . A national program may be sponsored by (Allied) Van Lines and their agents. It would be set up to bring college students or high school graduates into the business on an observing basis, which might stimulate interest. . . ."

Mr. Rolapp's interest in fighting high costs is a concern of every sensitive businesman in this country, for the high cost of doing business is making competitors' products more and more attractive in the American market.

Another industry leader is Hubert Work, Executive Vice President, The Weicker Transfer and Storage Company, Denver, Colorado, and Chairman of the Board of Allied Van Lines, Inc., who has said: "Allied Van Lines International Corporation has taken great strides since its inception. This growth in international shipments, within the past three years, has outstripped that of the industry as a whole—and probably most of the individual elements within the industry as well."

This need for international business imagination is coming at a time when our military alliances may become less entangling, and the number of families stationed with the military overseas would be far less than before. This condition too will make it necessary to look for more commercial household-goods business, rather than relying on military business, in the years ahead.

As a consideration of the future is so concerned with youth, it may seem highly incongruous to return, one final time, to Mrs. Kath Fetter of Chicago, who was so enthusiastic in her various interviews with this reporter. She is truly 76 years *young*, because she has not allowed her thought processes to grow stagnant. She is using her wisdom, and often using it for the benefit of younger people who must be considered the life blood of her business.

Without new blood, without the dedication of doing a good job, of performing a service to other people who need the moving and storage man or woman at the most critical time, there is no true picture conveyed about this industry. Mrs. Fetter is an inspiration in a time when some people are cynical about the future.

She has not "competed" over the years; she has "served." Countless young people are constantly asking their parents how they can get into a business that helps their fellow man. Mrs. Kath M. Fetter has the answer, in this reporter's view. She has found something that she has practiced with joy over 50 years' time. She serves as just one person, but a very important one in an industry that has dedicated itself to serving other peoples' needs.

No program for the future of the moving and storage industry could be complete without a strong desire on everyone's part within the industry to try to capture some of Mrs. Fetter's contagious enthusiasm, to serve a public that many feel is growing almost totally apathetic about its regard for the other fellow. Mrs. Fetter doesn't buy that philosophy.

In fact, almost every one of the many moving and storage men and women this interviewer has seen over the past two years projected this enthusiasm. They had love for the jobs they were doing. . . . And what greater pleasure can a person have than to enjoy his work . . . and try to make it better in the years ahead?

In the mobile society, there is growth. In growth, there is knowledge.

Index

Index